MW01712766

MAPLE SPOUTS SPILES & TAPS

Hale Mattoon

Flying Squirrel Press
Vershire, Vermont

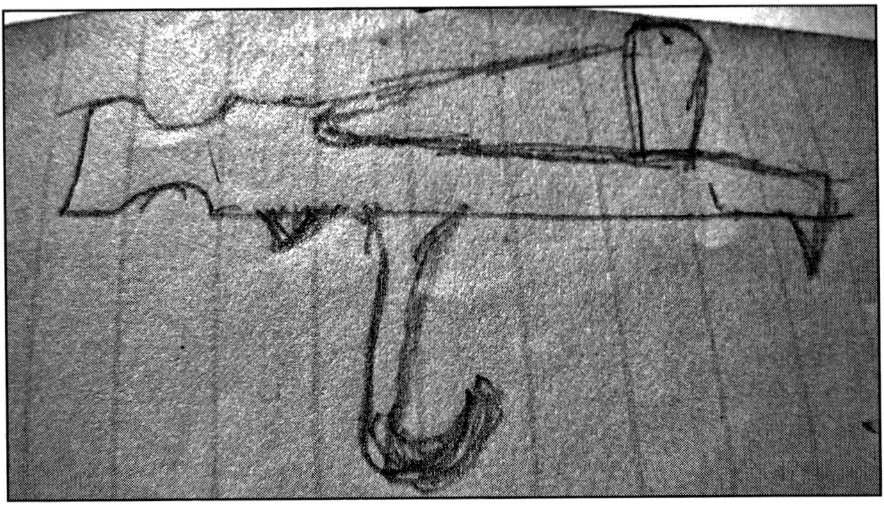

Courtesy of Mary Tebbetts

Cover illustration: The Tebbetts Spout, patented 1899

This sketch of the Tebbetts spout appears in
Edward J. Tebbetts' 1890 diary.

To mailorder one book, please send $14.50 to
Hale Mattoon, 274 East Randolph Road,
Chelsea, Vermont 05038
For more copies, write or email us for price.
dfm842@yahoo.com

ISBN 978-1-63068-049-7

DEDICATION

This book is dedicated to all past, present, and future maple sugar makers that have, do, and will continue to use the maple sap spout. It is also dedicated to those who have contributed through the years to make a good product better. Bless you all.

ACKNOWLEDGMENTS

Top of the list is Diane, my wife, confidante, clerical organizer, and supporter of this project from start to finish. Fred Webster planted the seed and inspired me to share the contents of this book with others. I am most grateful to John Douglas for his photographic knowledge, design expertise, and endless efforts to bring everything together. Your help on this project will never be forgotten. Thanks to Joan Waltermire for her sincere, forthcoming, and endless editorial input.

A very special thanks to those who allowed us to take photos of your spouts, spiles, printed matter, and spout-related items: Erwin Fullerton, Ted Greene, Gary Gaudette and Leader Evaporator Company, David Hauenstein III, Tom Olson, Pete and Mary Powers, Gerard and Sandy Stevens, and Mary Tebbetts.

INTRODUCTION

The evolution of extracting sap from the maple tree in the beginning with simple primitive tools was not a smooth process. The enthusiasm of the native North Americans, early settlers, and the maple sugar makers that followed through the years made continuous improvements in the quality of the sap and health of the tree. The horizon of the tapping endeavor was greatly extended with the use of wood, sheet metal, iron and modern plastic.

The hobby of collecting these interesting items that are used to transfer sap from the tree to a container or line for processing has spawned a variety of names for them: spouts, spiles, taps, spigots, collectors, and conveyors are a few. In this area of east central Vermont, they are called spouts by most, but if you travel in any direction where maple sugaring is done you will hear the other terms. My feeling is that no matter what these transferrers are called somewhere else, if it is a spile to you, call it a spile. If it is a spout to you, call it a spout. Keep the tradition alive.

Wooden spouts certainly add to any spout collection, but very little information is known about patents or the name of the manufacturer, as many, or most, were homemade.

The main emphasis of this book is the era of the mid-eighteen hundreds to the mid-nineteen hundreds. During this period there was revolutionary change in the making of equipment for maple sugaring. The sap spouts were certainly a part of this change as they went from wood to cast and formed metal.

There were many patents registered in the patent offices of the United States and Canada during this time, but some spouts were never patented. They were made in many shapes and sizes. Some were handmade and some machine-made; some were made of machine-formed sheet steel and some of molded metal. They were untreated or treated with galvanizing or tin coating. Some of them hardly look like a spout.

The flexible or plastic pipeline first patented in the nineteen-fifties required a completely different type of spout from that used with a pail or bucket. This has reduced the cost of labor and equipment, and has been a key to higher production in the making of maple syrup.

I hope this assemblage of material and photos will be a resource for anyone interested in the hobby of collecting maple sap spouts.

Section One

WOODEN SPOUTS

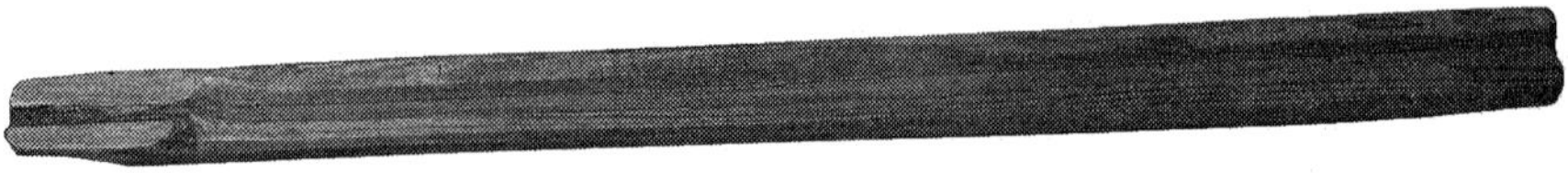

Handmade Pennsylvania wooden spout

This is 17" long and came from an old sugar house in Somerset County, PA. The author was given this spout by Dave Hauenstein III.

John McCombs
November 22, 1864 Patent

Edinburg, Ohio

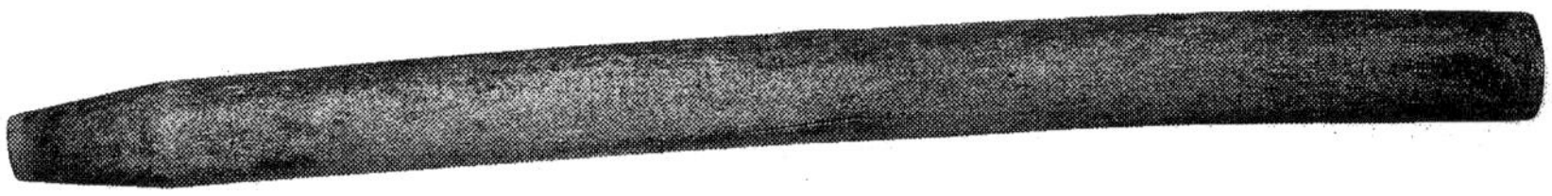

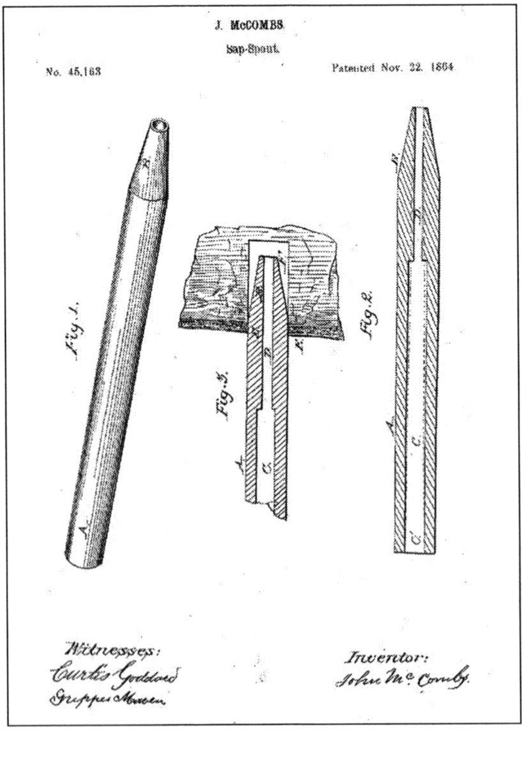

A variety of wooden spouts

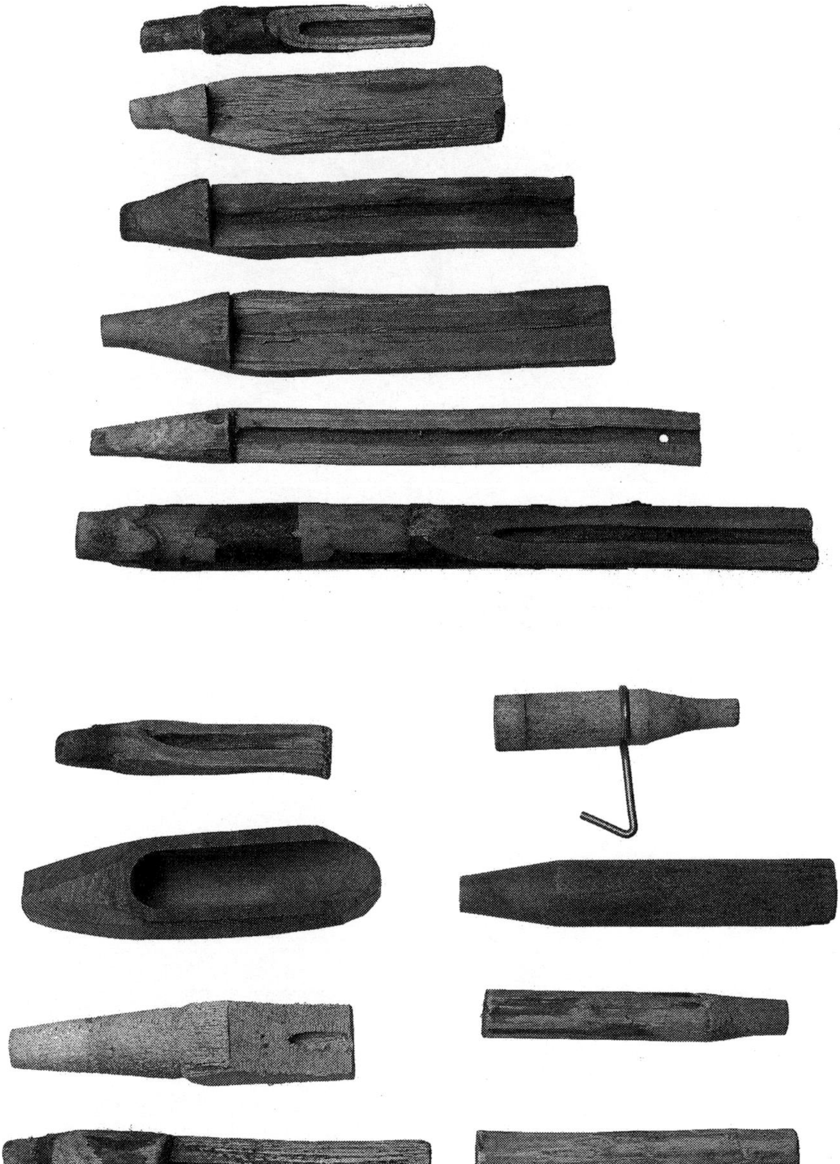

F.E. Lord
1887 Patent

Manufactured in Readsboro, Vermont

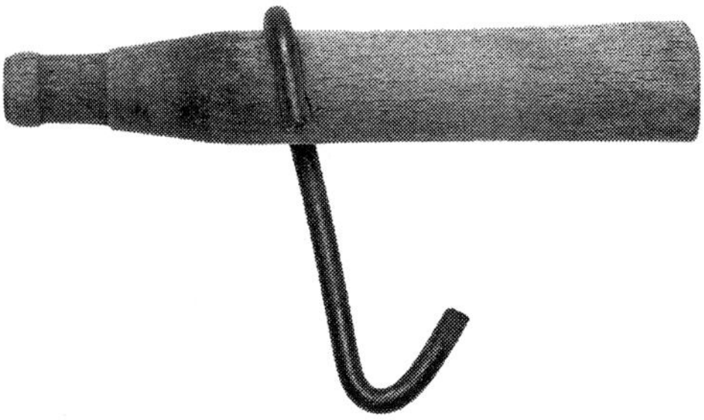

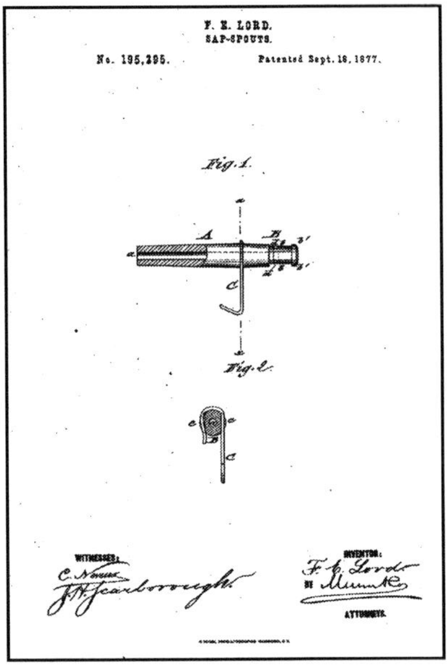

Ad courtesy of The New England Maple Museum

Section Two

METAL SPOUTS

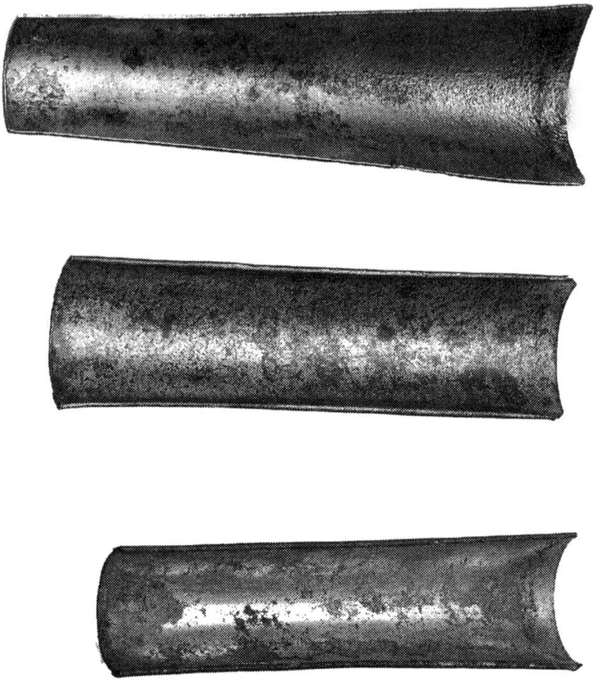

Open channel gouge spouts
Approximately 3"- 4" long

Small gouge tool and spout

Rolled tin sap spout, semi-open channel

Rolled tin spouts with tubular barrels

The boys and their spouts

"Some 100 years ago Sylvester (Vet) Thompson had his tin shop in Edson Rowland's cellar, he sometimes worked all night. Here he made by hand sap spouts, sap buckets, heaters, sap pans, sugarpans, dish pans, sugar tins and tin water pails. Vet used to give his waste tin to three boys, Charles Page, Frank Corliss, and Hale Darling. The boys made 100 spouts from the waste tin and sold them for $1.00. The money, of course, was divided equally, each having 33 cents, with one cent left over. How should they divide one cent among three? After much deliberation they decided to buy a stick of peppermint candy, divide the candy in three parts, and thus solve the problem."

Taken from the Town of Corinth, Vermont History 1764-1964
Courtesy of the Selectboard of the Town of Corinth, Vermont

Sap Nails

Sap nails were used to hang buckets from trees when early wooden gouge and tin spouts were used.

"Some of the first metal sap spouts were only round pieces of tin. Trees were tapped by boring a hole and cleaning the bark from the area around it. A sap spout was then inserted beneath the hole and under that a nail was driven to hold the wooden sap bucket. Charles Page of East Corinth made sap nails in his village blacksmith shop from the backs of old scythe blades. Joe Longry, a jolly old Frenchman, often stopped at the blacksmith shop to pass the time of day with Charles. Joe would light his old clay pipe from a red hot nail on which Charles was working. Thus Joe saved a match and had a good visit to boot."

Taken from the Town of Corinth, Vermont History 1764-1964
Courtesy of the Selectboard of the Town of Corinth, Vermont

Section Three

VERMONT SPOUTS

R.F. Livermore
1868 Patent

Starksboro, Vermont

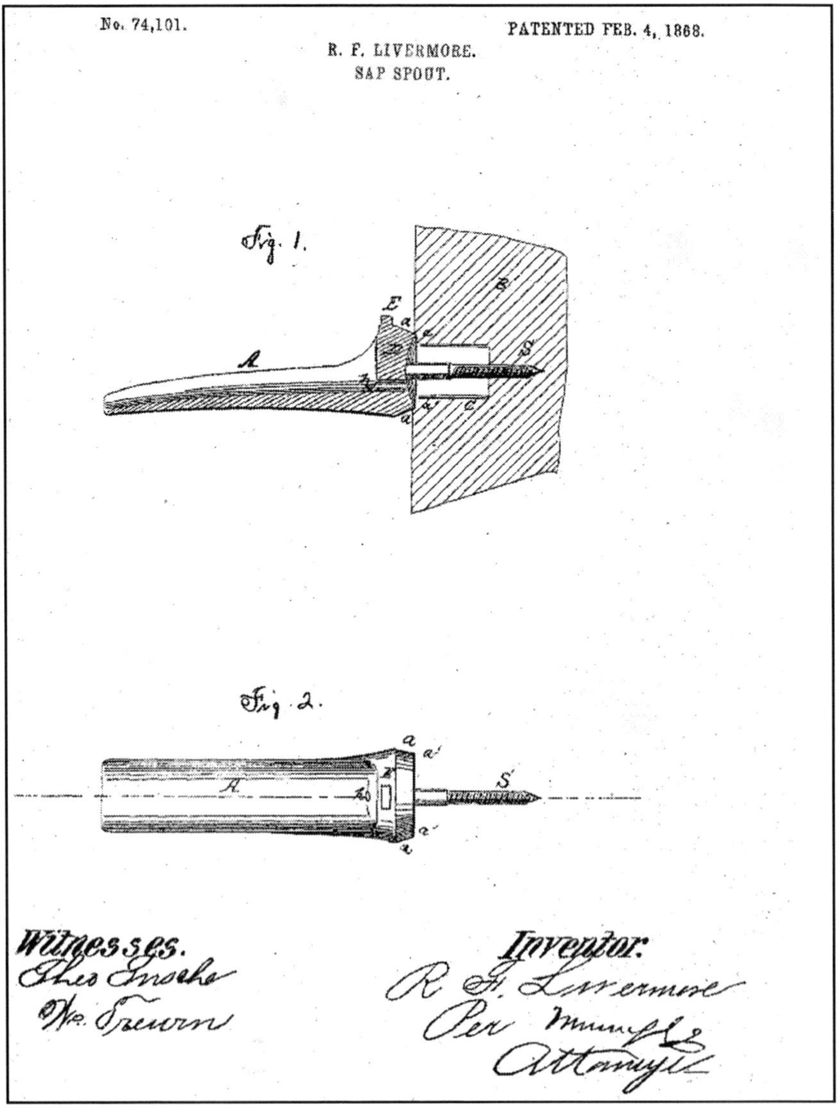

C.C. Post

"The Eureka"

1868 Patent

Burlington, Vermont

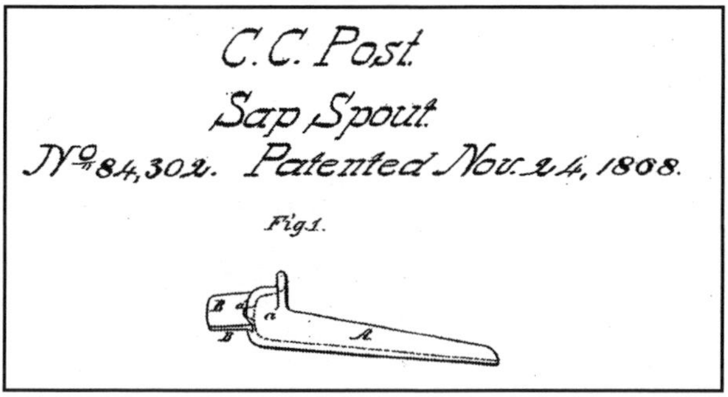

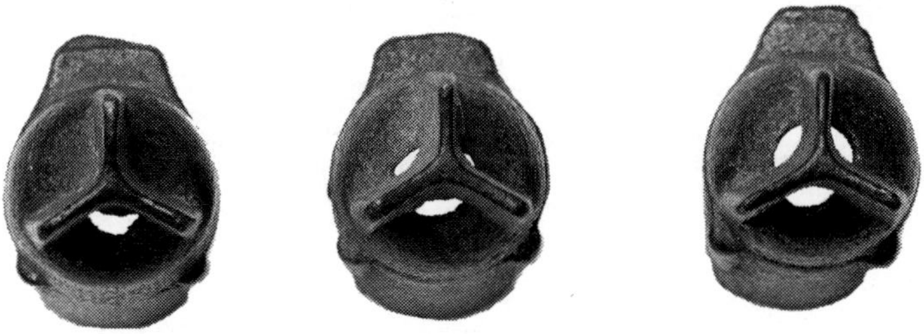

Inlet hole variations

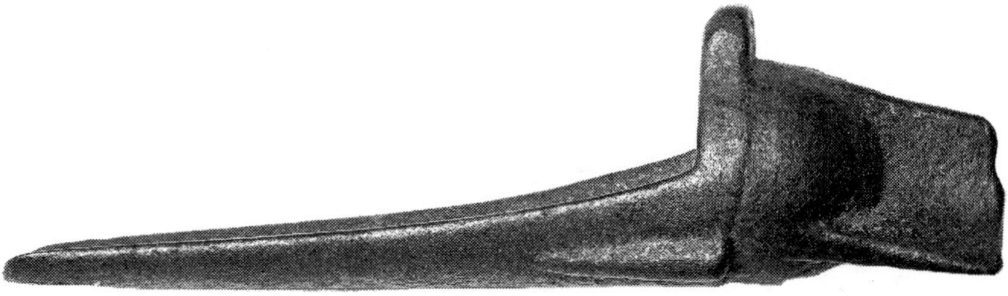

Side view showing boss lines

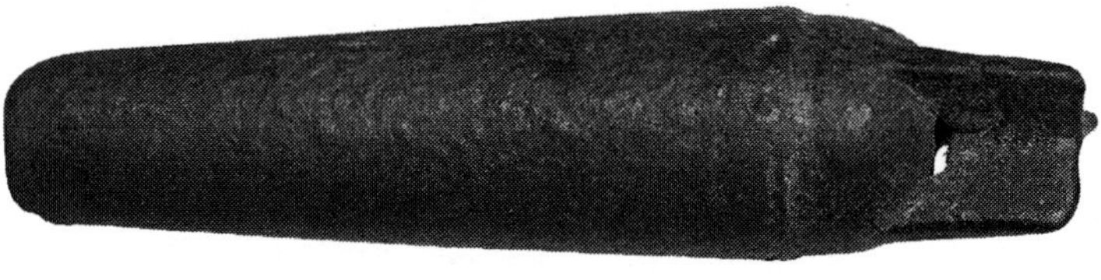

Bottom smooth with no boss lines

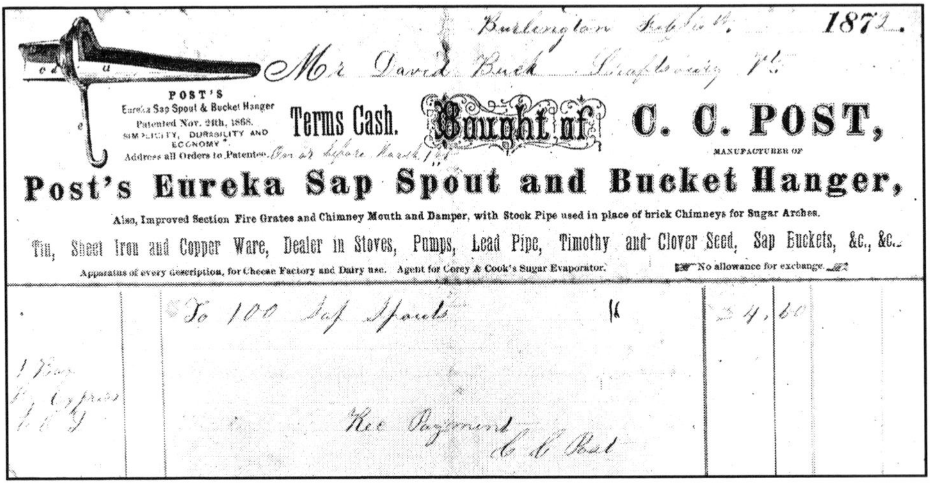

Burlington 1872

Mr David Buck

POST'S
Eureka Sap Spout & Bucket Hanger
Patented Nov. 24th, 1868.
SIMPLICITY, DURABILITY AND ECONOMY.
Address all Orders to Patentee.

Terms Cash. Bought of C. C. POST,

MANUFACTURER OF

Post's Eureka Sap Spout and Bucket Hanger,

Also, Improved Section Fire Grates and Chimney Mouth and Damper, with Stock Pipe used in place of brick Chimneys for Sugar Arches.

Tin, Sheet Iron and Copper Ware, Dealer in Stoves, Pumps, Lead Pipe, Timothy and Clover Seed, Sap Buckets, &c., &c.

Apparatus of every description, for Cheese Factory and Dairy use. Agent for Corey & Cook's Sugar Evaporator. No allowance for exchange.

To 100 Sap Spouts $4.60

Rec Payment C C Post

Billhead courtsey of The New England Maple Museum

Examples of type 1 and type 2 of the 1868 patent

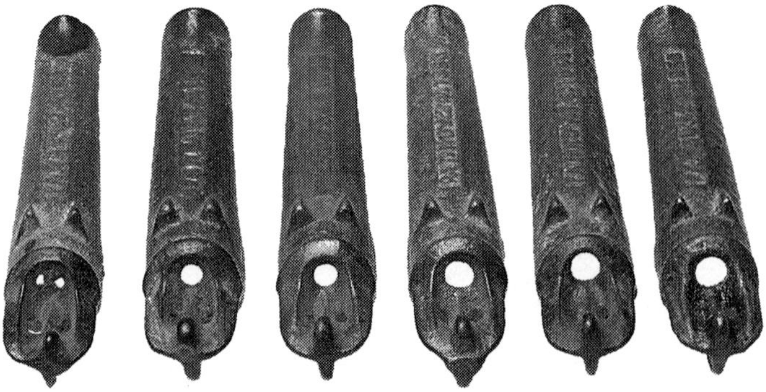

Type 2 spouts with 6 size variations of inlet hole

C.C. Post
"The Eureka"
1872 Patent

Hinesburg, Vermont

Two casting variations of the 1872 patent

The bottom spout required a wire hook.

The top spout has a slot to hold the bucket on each side of the channel.

Side view of the same spouts

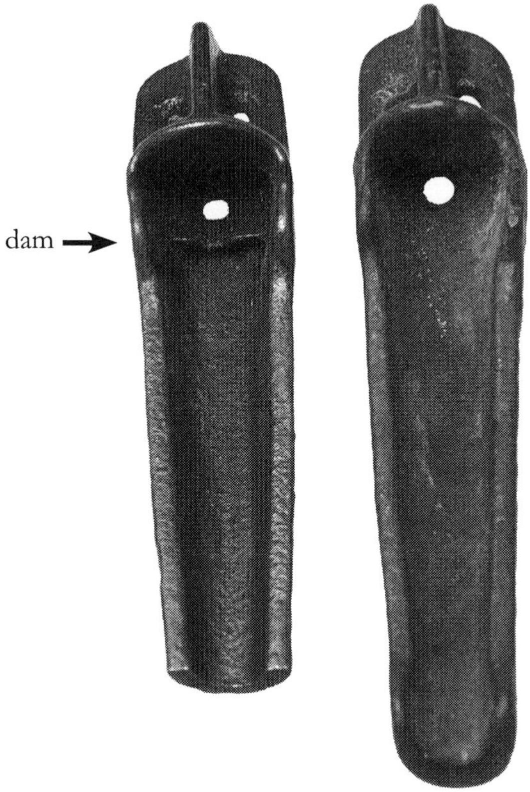

Left: Rare version of the 1872 patent with a dam
The dam held back enough sap to keep the tap hole from drying out when the weather was not favorable for a sap flow. All 1884 patent spouts would have dams.

Right: Typical 1872 patent spout without a dam

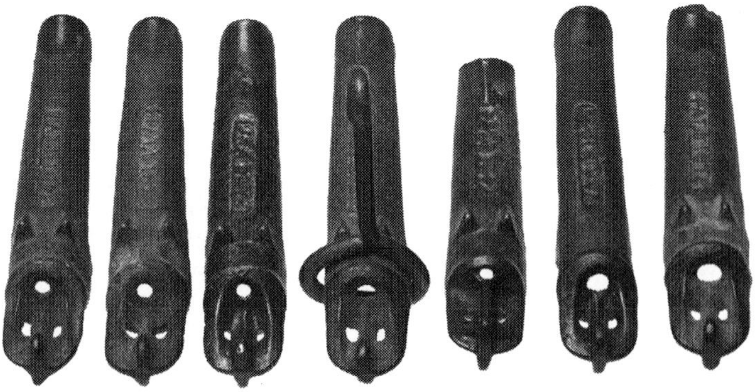

Variations of the 1872 patent
Notice the hole sizes and spout lengths.

C.C. Post
"The Eureka"
1884 Patent

Burlington, Vermont

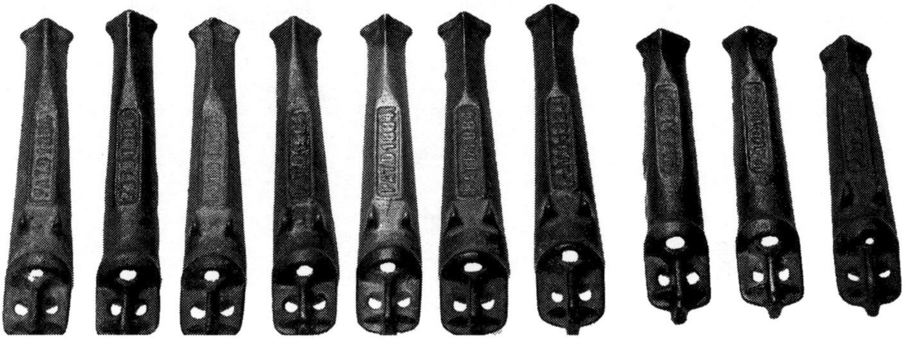

Variations of the 1884 patent

VERMONT FARM MACHINE COMPANY, BELLOWS FALLS, VT. 13

SAP SPOUTS

Eureka Galvanized Sap Spouts.

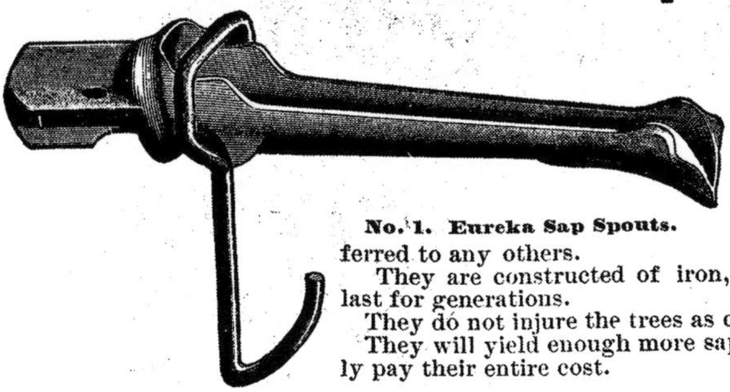

No. 1. Eureka Sap Spouts.

These popular spouts are too well known among the best sugar makers to require a lengthy description of their advantages. We give a few reasons why they are preferred to any others.

They are constructed of iron, galvanized and will last for generations.

They do not injure the trees as other spouts do.

They will yield enough more sap every year to doubly pay their entire cost.

They will run earlier and later in the day and later in the season.

They have the most convenient hanging for any style of bucket.

Their construction is such as not to obstruct the flow of the sap from the outer pores as do wood spouts.

There have been more than 14,000,000 of the Eureka Sap Spouts sold.

PRICES.

No. 1, with wire Hanger, per 100,	$3.00.
No. 2, without " " " "	2.50.

1884 patent spouts that supported the bucket without needing a hook

Spouts from the same patent that required a hook to hang buckets

Both were available in 3 ¼" and 2 ¾" lengths.

No. 29. Post's Eureka Sap Spouts.

Made by C. C. Post, Burlington, Vt. These sap spouts have been in use for many years, and have always given the best of satisfaction. They are made from the best quality of iron, and are galvanized. They do not rust or corrode, and will last for generations. They do not injure the tree, and are more quickly adjusted than any others. No sugar maker can afford to do without them. The price of

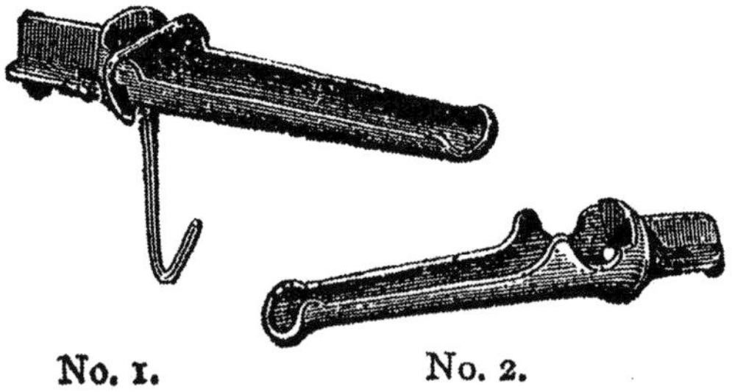

No. 1. No. 2.

these spouts is $4.50 per hundred (see cuts 1 and 2). It will be observed that No. 1 has a hook for the support of the buckets and No. 2 is designed for buckets that have ears to them, which slip over the end of the spout, and are firmly held by the grooves in the spout. We give 100 of either style of these spouts for a club of 14 subscribers at $2.00 each.

Ad for 1872 patent Eureka spouts

The 1884 patent spouts also showed variations in the orientation of the inlet hole. The 2 ¾" hookless spout above has a horizontal inlet hole.

This rare 2 ¾" hook spout has a vertical inlet hole.

Charles C. Post's sap spouts

Early in the 1860s Mr. C. C. Post realized that there were drawbacks to using wooden spouts, and that sugar-making could be improved by using a metal spout. In 1868, Mr. Post was issued a patent on a spout design called Post's Eureka Sap Spout. Mr. Post made improvements in his Eureka Spout and received more patents in 1872 and 1884. By 1892, he had sold over 14,000,000 spouts.

In 1912, when Mr. Post decided he did not want to continue in the active business of making spouts, he sold his interest to Mr. Charles C. Stelle. Mr. Stelle made improvements to, patented, and continued to manufacture the Eureka spout.

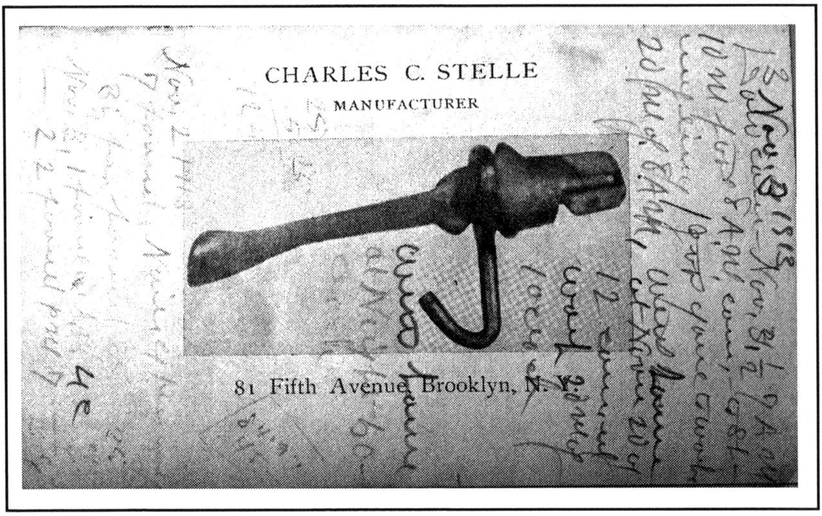

Availability of Eureka sap spouts

The Vermont Farm Machine Company of Bellows Falls, Vermont, did not manufacture sap spouts, but it did list available spouts in the following catalogs. Prices were not given in the 1919 catalog.

1892

Eureka No. 1 with hanger	$3.00 per 100
Eureka No. 2 without hanger	$2.50 per 100

1903

Eureka No. 1 with hanger	$2.50 per 100
Eureka No. 2 without hanger	$2.25 per 100

1905

Eureka No. 1 with hanger	$2.25 per 100
Eureka No. 2 without hanger	$1.75 per 100

1919

Improved Stelle (The Eureka) Sap Spout	No price given

Charles C. Stelle
"The Eureka"
1912 Patent
Brooklyn, New York

Side and bottom view of the 1912 patent

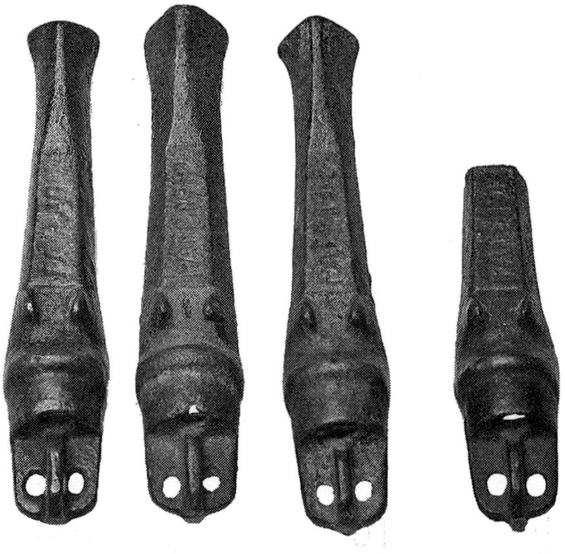

Variations of the 1912 Stelle patent

It is not known whether or not the short spout on the right was marketed like this, or if it was simply cut off by an individual. However, such short Stelle spouts appear in many locations in New England, so it is possible that it was deliberately produced in this form.

Lorin Tabor
1892 Patent

Westford, Vermont

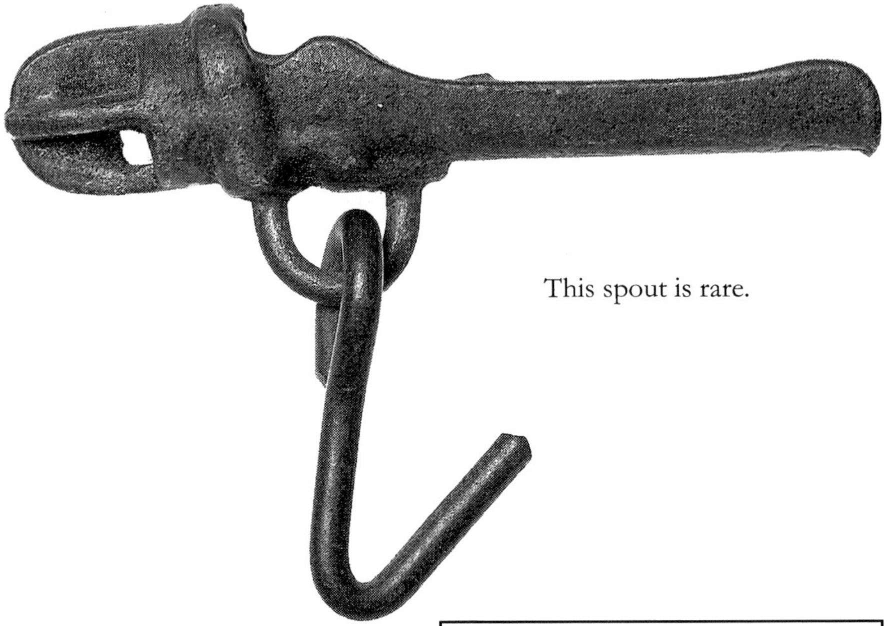

This spout is rare.

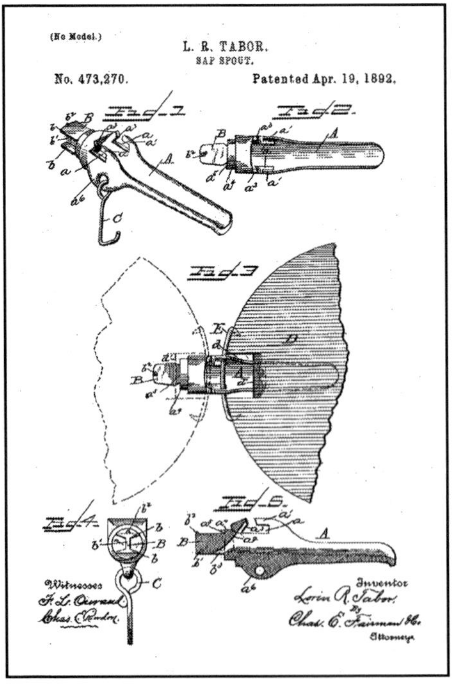

J.W. Currier
1892 Patent

North Troy, Vermont

(No Model.)

J. W. CURRIER.

SAP SPOUT.

No. 469,232. Patented Feb. 23, 1892.

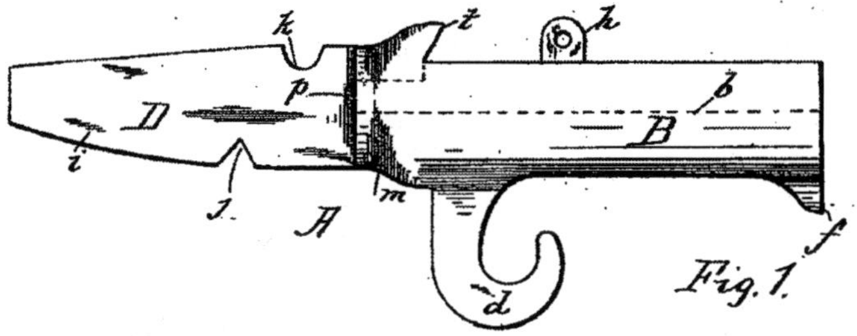

This spout was patented by J.W. Currier and marketed by the Joseph Breck Company of Boston, Massachusetts.

BRECK'S SAP SPOUTS.

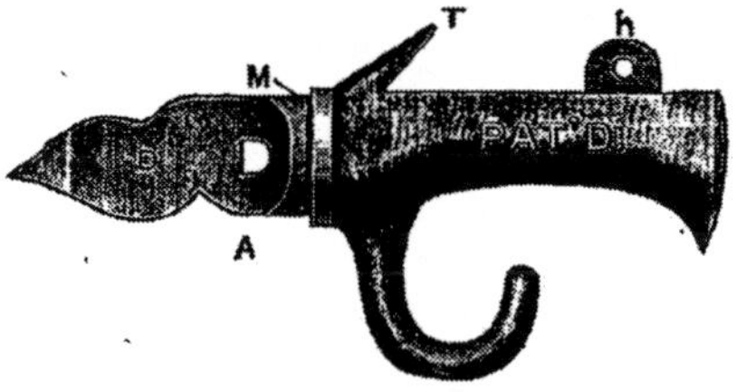

This is the invention of a practical sugar maker and is without doubt the most efficient device for collecting the maple sap ever offered. It is a well known fact that the sap lies within an inch of the bark, and a careful examination of the most approved spouts on the market will reveal the fact that in order to have the spout sustain the weight of the sap bucket and contents, the spout must be driven into the tree, thereby closing the grain, and preventing the flow of sap. The Breck spout excels all others in this respect, securing the entire flow of sap or fully a third more than any other.

The sap-hole is bored in the tree in the usual manner, the spout A is inserted therein, driving the point of its blade D slightly into the body of the tree at the bottom of the hole. The reduced portion M of the spout-body enters that portion of the hole surrounded by the bark of the tree, and forms a bearing for the spout. By this means the grain of the wood is in no manner compressed by the spout when inserted in the sap-hole, the only bearing of the spout in the tree being the point of the blade at the bottom of the hole and the reduced body portion in the bark.

The Breck spout being made from the best galvanized malleable iron is indestructible. From good authority there is at least twenty to twenty-five per cent. breakage from driving the common cast iron spouts in present use and a large loss of sap caused by the buckets twisting the hooks off, the hooks not being made so as to withstand the strain of high winds. It is impossible for this loss to occur when the Breck sprouts are used.

Breck's Sap Spouts . . . . Our net price, per 100 spouts, $2.50

J. W. Currier patent, 1892, casting variations

Type 1
Raised letters and PAT-D
Slotted eye, 7⁄16" wide at eye of the tip end, short bar

Galvanized, 2 15⁄16" long

Iron, 2 7⁄8" long

Casting variations
Type 2
Small raised letters PAT'D
Galvanized, 2 15⁄16" long, 7⁄16" wide at eye of the tip end

Small D inlet hole

Large D inlet hole

Type 2 casting variations, continued
Small raised letters PAT'D
2 ⅞" long, $\frac{7}{16}$" wide at eye of the tip end

Iron, medium D inlet hole

Galvanized, large D inlet hole

J. W. Currier patent, 1892, continued

Type 2, casting variations continued
Small raised letters PAT'D, 7⁄16" wide at the eye, galvanized

Small D inlet hole, 2 15⁄16" long

Small round inlet hole, 2 7⁄8" long

J. W. Currier patent, 1892, casting variations

Type 3
Recessed letters PAT-D, 5⁄16" wide at the eye of the tip end

Galvanized, 2 ¾" long

Iron, 2 13⁄16 " long

Iron, 2 13⁄16 " long, extra large D inlet hole

James F. Warner
1893 Patent

Essex, Vermont

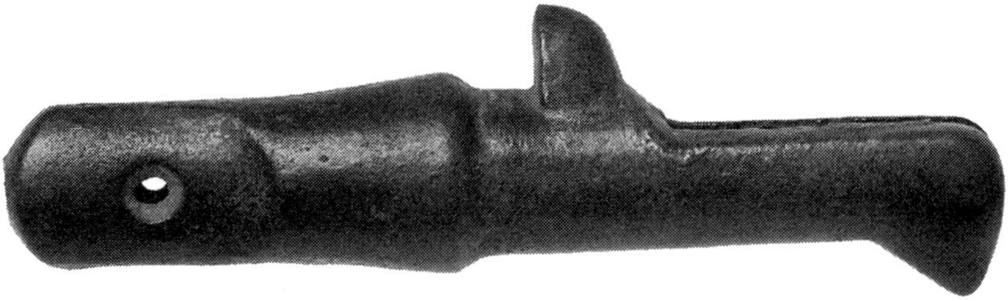

The spout must be turned upside down to read the patent date.
See page 48 for a description of an interesting 1893 patent variation.

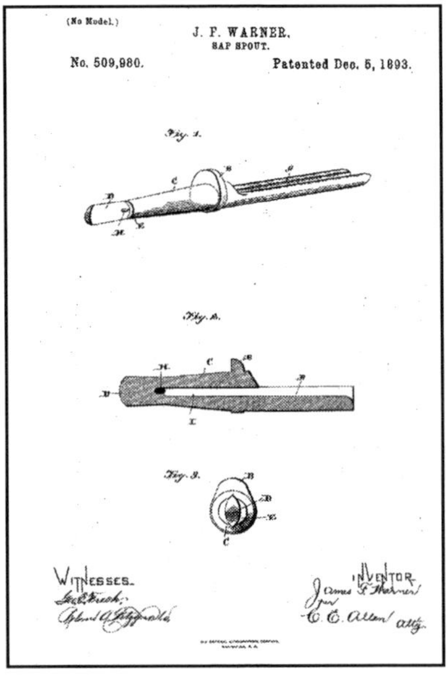

James F. Warner
1899 Patent

Essex, Vermont

There are no identification markings on this spout. It is believed to be the J. F. Warner 1899 patent.

James F. Warner
1903 Patent applied for

Small block letters PAT.APLD. on one side (shown on both spouts); WARNER on the reverse; both are uncommon

Straight barrel, 2 ¾" long

Arched barrel, 2 ⅝" long

It was a problem to hang and remove the bucket on the short arched Warner because there was so little clearance between the tip of the hook and the drip end of the spout.

James F. Warner
1903 Patent

Essex, Vermont

Iron, 2 ⅝" long, raised letters and numbers

Arched, PATD. 03 showing; WARNER on the reverse

Arched, WARNER showing; PATD. 03 on the reverse

Straight, PATD. 03 showing; WARNER on the reverse

Straight, WARNER showing; PATD. 03 on the reverse

James F. Warner
1904 Patent

Essex, Vermont

Hookless Warner spouts with recessed letters, different combs, PAT-D on side showing; WARNER on the reverse; ⅛" to ⅜" in spacing between T and D

Iron

Iron

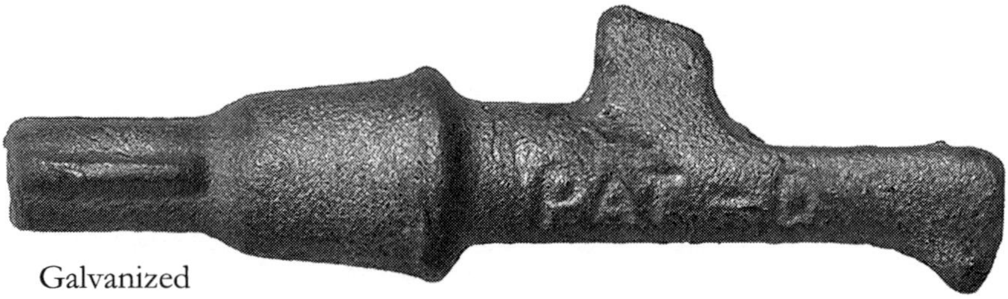

Galvanized

Iron

GEO. D. JARVIS JAMES F. WARNER

GEO. D. JARVIS & CO.
MANUFACTURERS OF
THE WARNER SAP SPOUT,
BUCKET-COVERS & SUGAR MAKER'S SUPPLIES

45 CHURCH ST. BURLINGTON, VT. Jan 30/09.

J. K. Burlingame,

Boonville, N.Y.

Dear Sir:

We are enclosing you a catalogue of the Warner Sap Spout which we trust you will read as every sugar-dealer is desirous of obtaining all the information possible regarding the flow of sap. We claim that the Warner Sap Spout produces more sap than any other spout manufactured and is the only perfect spout on the market. It is made of malleable iron and will not break.

If after reading the catalogue and the testimonials therein, you are convinced that we have something different from anyone else, we would be pleased to have you try a few and watch the results this season. They will be for sale in your town by the merchant whose name appears on this catalogue. He will not only carry the Warner Sap Spout but the Warner bucket, tapping bit, sugar pails, syrup cans and everything in the sugar-makers line and will be pleased to show them to you and receive your patronage. We are sure that if you once use the Warner spout, you will never use any other.

We trust that we will be able to add your name to our list of many satisfied customers.

Very truly yours,

Geo. D. Jarvis & Co.

Dict.GDJ/CVE.

James F. Warner and George Jarvis
1905 Patent

Warner of Essex; Jarvis of Burlington

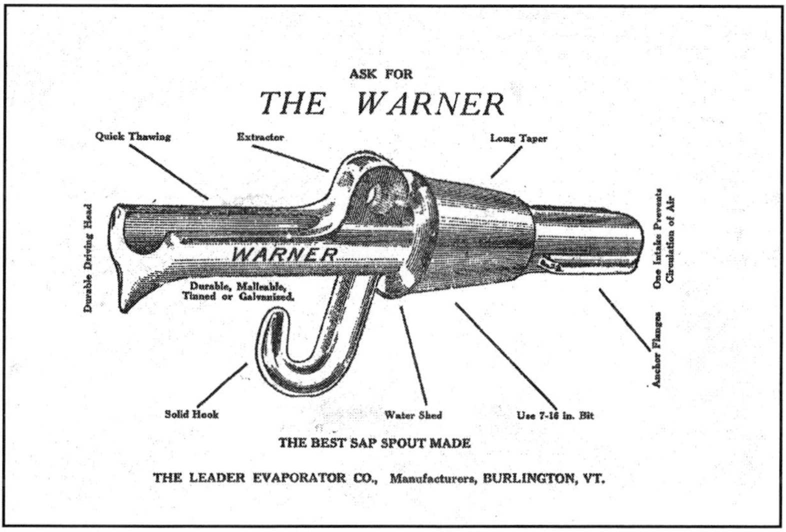

Uncommon

Recessed letters PAT-D, X on the apex, 2 ⅞" long; WARNER on the reverse.

Warner-Jarvis, 1905 Patent, variations

Iron, letters recessed

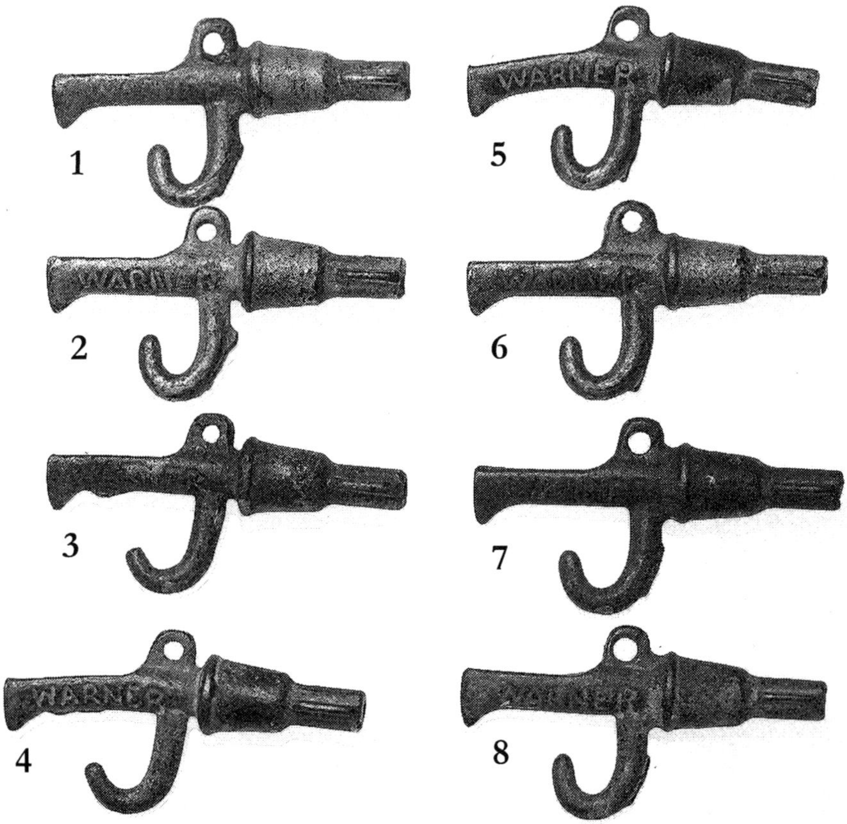

1 Common Warner

2 Deep valley eye

3 Deep valley eye; casting mark under WARNER

4 Arched; deep valley eye; casting mark under WARNER

5 Arched; casting mark on hook

6 High-set eye; heavy casting

7 PAT-D lacking on reverse

8 Very large eye

Warner-Jarvis, 1905 Patent, variations

Galvanized

Solid barrel spouts with variation in apex flanges
Letters recessed, WARNER showing with PAT-D on reverse

heavy flange

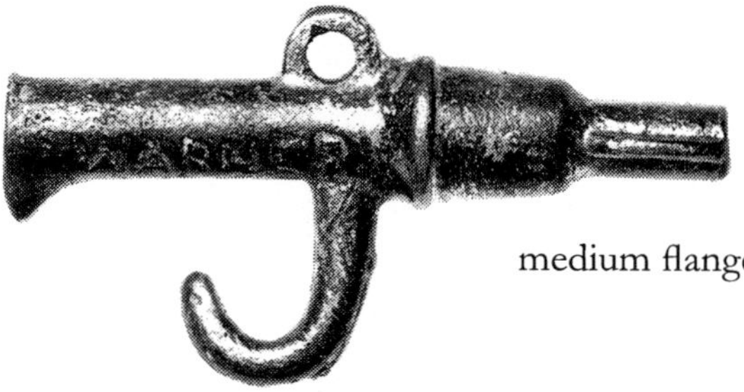

medium flange

thin flange

Alonzo Foster
1894 Patent

Cabot, Vermont

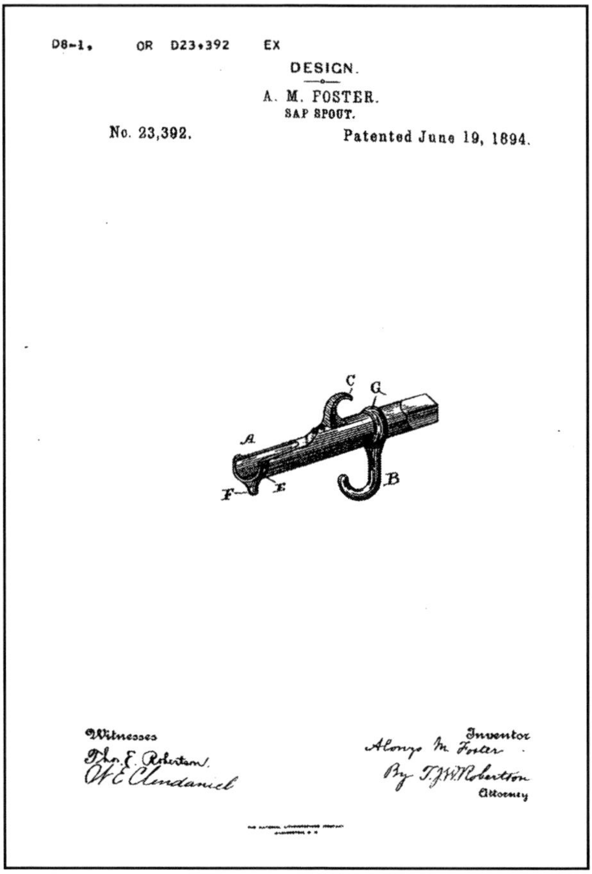

D8-1. OR D23,392 EX

DESIGN.

A. M. FOSTER.

SAP SPOUT.

No. 23,392. Patented June 19, 1894.

Witnesses
Thos. F. Robertson.
W. E. Clendaniel

Alonzo M. Foster Inventor
By T. J. W. Robertson
Attorney

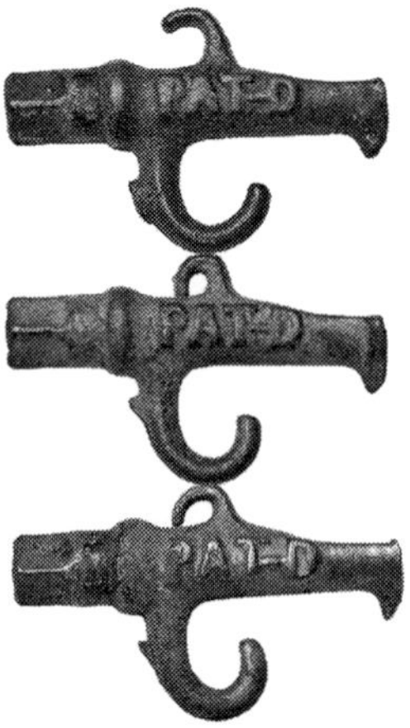

Variations, Type 1
Long bar, raised letters

Top: galvanized, small shoulder ring
Middle: iron, small shoulder ring
Bottom: galvanized, large shoulder ring

Variations, Type 3
Recessed letters

Variations, Type 2

Large shoulder rings,
short bar, raised letters

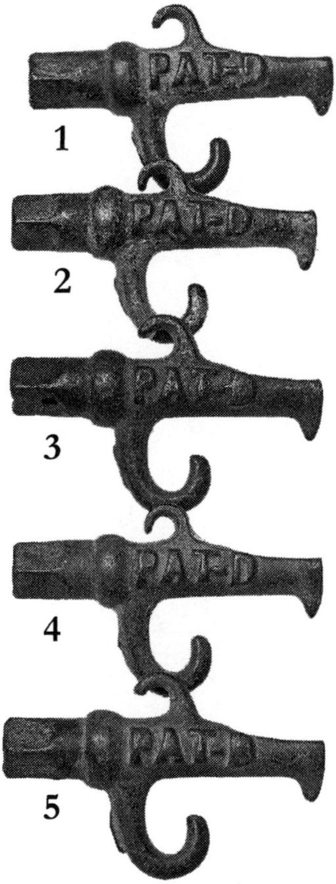

Bar may be present or missing (PAT-D or PATD); length from PAT-D to inlet tip of apex 1 15⁄16" to 2 1⁄4"; material iron or galvanized; shoulders large or small

Numbers 1 - 4 are iron; number 5 is galvanized.
Number 3 has two small inlet holes on the side.
Bar length and PAT-D length are different.

Alonzo Foster, 1894 Patent, continued
Variations, Type 4

Recessed letters, two inlet holes on side of apex

Length from PAT-D to inlet tip of apex variable; material iron or galvanized

Edward J. Tebbetts
1899 Patent

Lower Cabot, Vermont

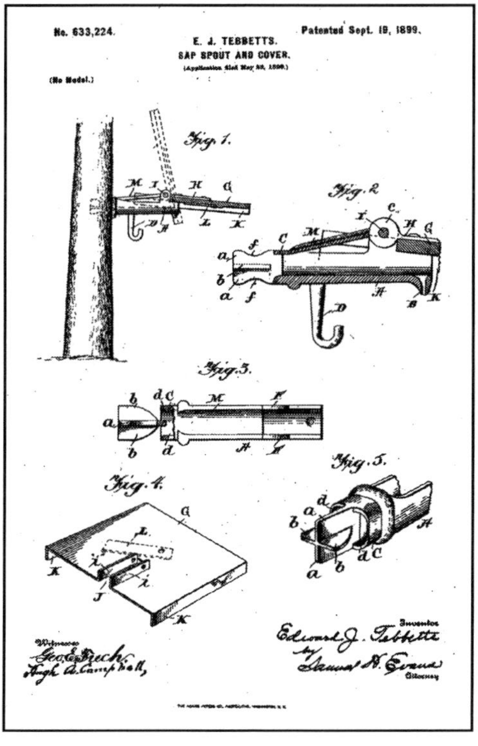

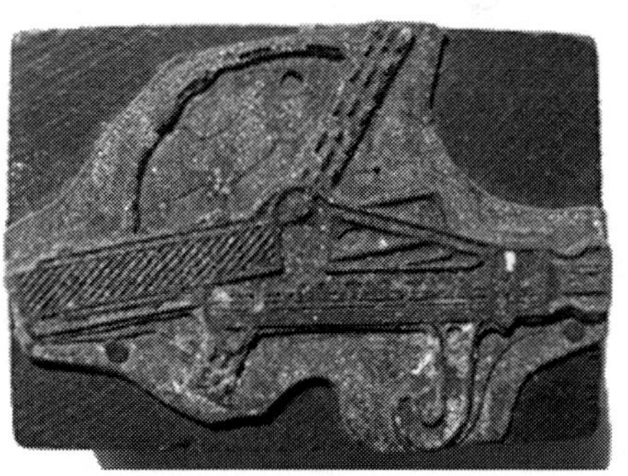

Courtesy of Mary Tebbetts

Printing block of spout design, used in correspondence

G. H. Grimm
July 19, 1904 Patent
Rutland, Vermont

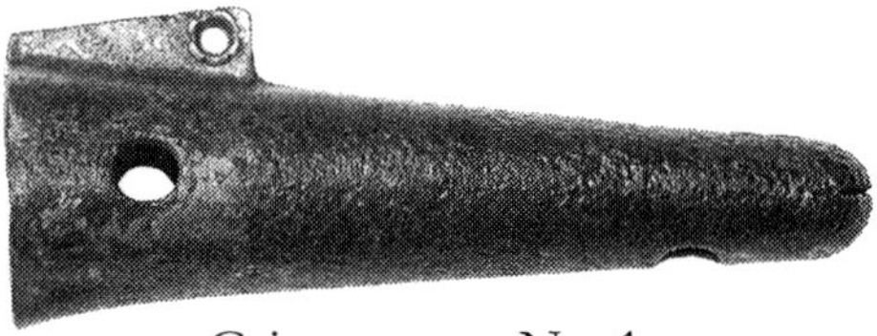

Grimm spout No. 1

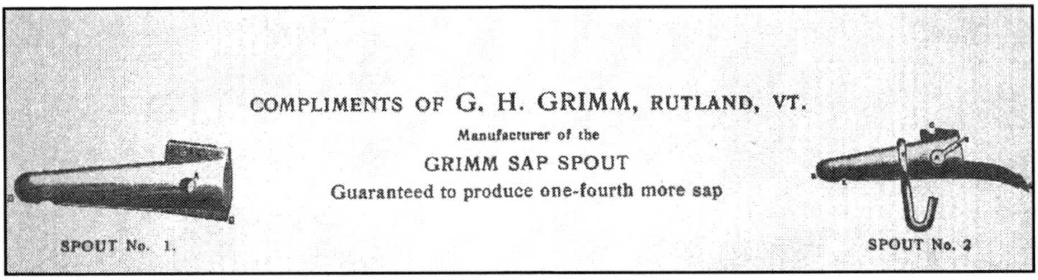

G. H. Grimm
Dec. 20, 1904 Patent
(spouts No. 2,3,4,5)

Grimm spout No. 3

Ad for a No. 3 Grimm spout in the 1905-06 Rutland Business Directory

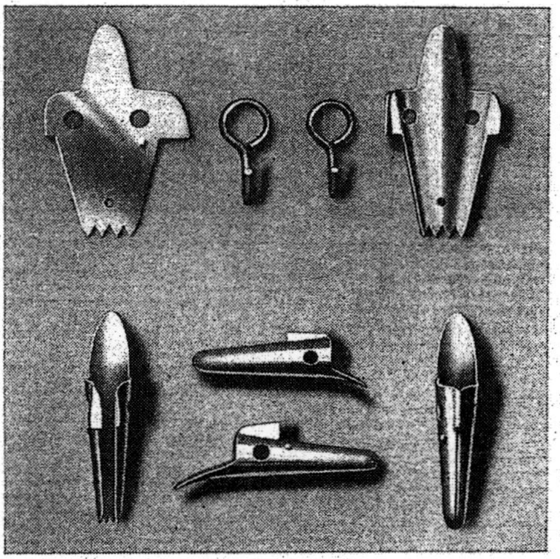

Grimm spout No. 4 without hook

Ads on this page are from the G. H. Grimm Catalog of Maple Sugar Makers' Equipment, dated early-to-middle thirties.

G. H. Grimm, Dec. 20, 1904 Patent, continued

The Grimm Sap Spout No. 5, Without Hook

Patented in United States and Canada

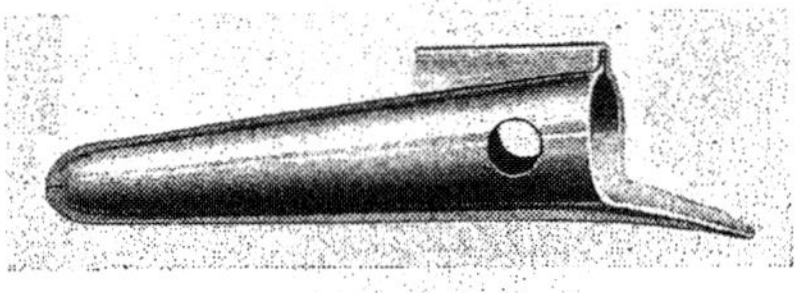

The Grimm Sap Spout No. 5 will fit a ⅜ inch bore without overlapping in driving. It is especially designed for use with buckets hung directly on the spout, but can also be used with a hook. This Spout, No. 5, will fit the ⅞ inch holes already punched in your buckets for the old style tin spouts.

THE Grimm Sap Spout provides all these ideal features and many more of equal importance. It is formed from a single piece of sheet steel in dies which are perfectly round and smooth, and it is coated with a material that will not rust.

The flap or lug on the upper side of the Grimm spout which holds the bucket or bucket hook in place is *formed with three thicknesses of steel, one of which over-laps the other, giving ample strength for driving and removing from the bore.*

The drip at the large end of the Grimm sap spout insures quick discharge and prevents the sap from running backward on the under side of the spout and going to waste.

The Grimm spout is easily withdrawn from the bore by passing a heavy wire nail or spike through the holes and turning it to the right or left, leaving the bark in such condition that the wound will heal in one season.

Being made of sheet steel, the Grimm spout starts earlier in the morning and runs later at night than any cast-iron or wooden spout.

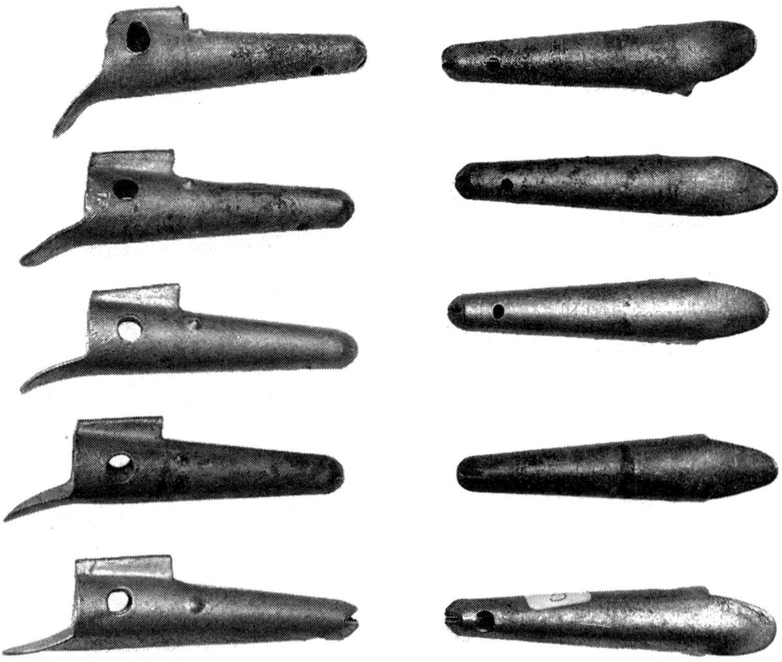

Side and bottom views of Grimm No. 5 spouts showing variations of the combs, removal and inlet holes

G. H. Grimm
1903 Canadian Patent

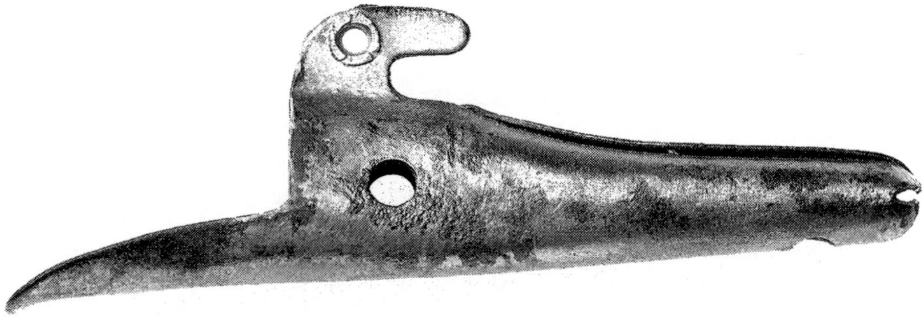

Spout drivers

Spout drivers are fitted into the open end of a spout to keep it from being deformed when driven in with a hammer.

Damaged spout hammered without a driver

Spout protected by using the spout driver shown below.

Spout driver

The Vermont Spout
No patent found

The Vermont spout differs from the Grimm spout in the structure of its comb. The Grimm comb was asymmetrical (see ad on page 39). This allowed the longer side to be bent over the shorter to make a triple thickness. It was not soldered. On the Vermont spout, the two identical sides of the comb were not folded, but were soldered.

The Vermont sap spout manufactured of cold rolled steel and then dipped to obtain a tin coating. This spout is favored by some producers. Available in two sizes for the 7/16″ tap and 3/8″ tap.

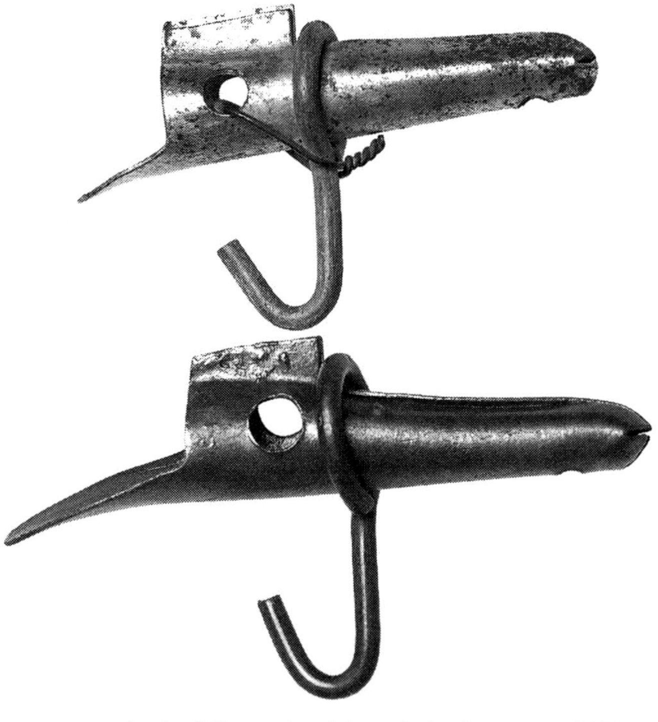

The top spout required a 3/8" tapping bit and the bottom a 7/16" tapping bit.

The Vermont spout was originally manufactured in Rutland, Vermont, in the 1920s by the Vermont Evaporator Company. After a fire, its manufacture shifted to St. Regis Falls, New York, and then to Ogdensburg, New York. In 1972, Leader Evaporator Company of St. Albans, Vermont, purchased the Vermont Evaporator Company.

G. H. Soule
1913 Patent

Fairfield, Vermont

Raised letters, SOULE showing, PATD on reverse

Cast iron, eight variations

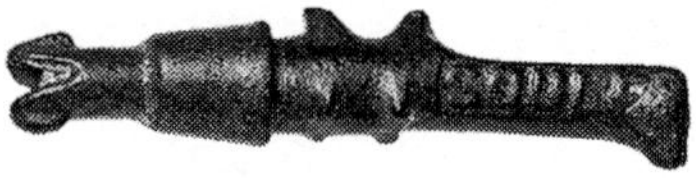

Reverse

Very rare open channel, SOULE cast on bottom

Soule and Warner spouts, aluminum alloy, as offered in the 1991 Leader Evaporator catalog

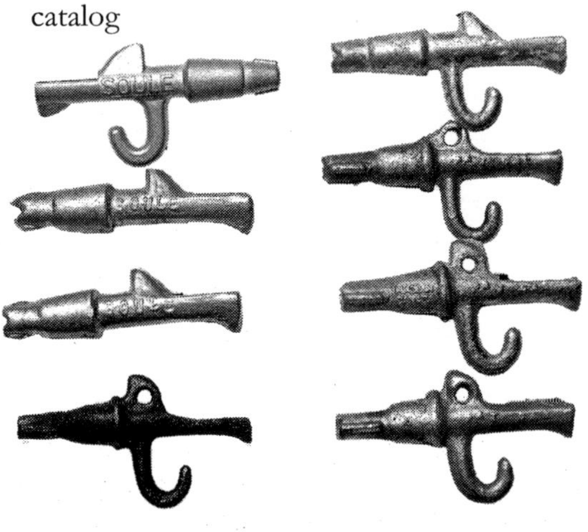

THE WARNER SPOUT

A long time favorite of the Sugar Maker, the WARNER Spout is available in the hooked style.

The spouts are made of aluminum alloy or malleable iron.

THE SOULE SPOUT

The SOULE Spout like the WARNER is manufactured of aluminum alloy or malleable iron.

G. H. Soule

Canadian patent

Letters recessed, SOULE showing, PATD CANADA on reverse

C.E. Whitcomb
1915 Patent
Richford, Vermont

Letters recessed, PAT. 3-26-15 showing

Early version
Tin coated, hookless with boss, bottom view

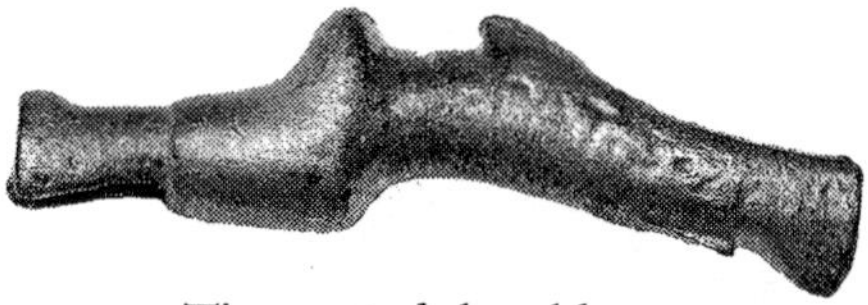

Tin coated, hookless

Galvanized, hookless

Galvanized, with hook

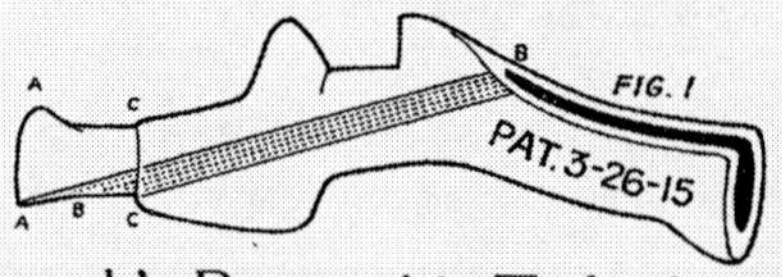

Whitcomb's Patent Air Tight Sap Spout.

This Spout, we think, supersedes all others. You will see at a glance at the hole in the spout that as soon as the sap begins to flow the air is excluded from the fresh cut tap, thereby forming a perfect Air Trap. This principle has been partially attained by all sorts of methods, but never in so simple a manner as this. This positively holds the bore full of sap, prevents the drying up of the pores, makes reaming unnecessary and prolongs the flow of sap to the very end of the season.

Points to be considered when buying a sap spout are:—1st. One that will best keep the air from coming into contact with the fresh cut wood. 2nd. Convenience in handling. 3d. One that will not leak. 4th. Durability. 5th. One that will keep sweet the longest. 6th. One that will harm the tree the least. 7th. One that will make it easy for, and not delay the sap gatherer by being obliged to take the bucket down in order to empty same, and one most suitable for a bucket cover. (This spout is also made with a hook to meet the demands of the sugar maker who is equipped for this style only.)

We believe we have such a spout. If you will examine the cut (Fig. 1) you will note the different points referred to. aa and cc are the only portions of the spout that comes in contact with the tree; it is held steady and does not close any of the sap-giving grains of the tree. bb gives you some idea how the hole is constructed.

We would like to have you try these spouts. It is not our intention to mislead anyone; we want you to try them, that is all, though 50 or 100 is few enough to test fairly. Read the following testimonials and see what good reliable parties say about this spout.

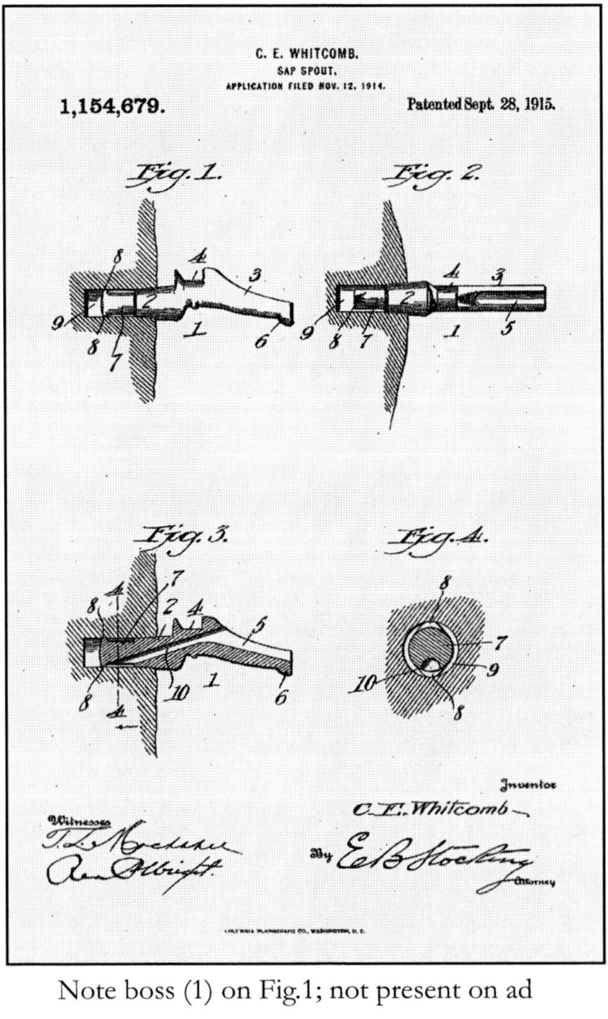

Note boss (1) on Fig.1; not present on ad

L.S. Blood
1921 Patent

Hartland, Vermont

Sap gathering extension

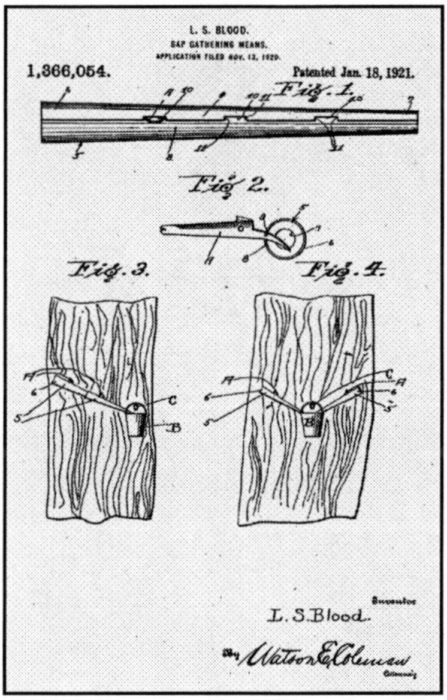

R.E. Caswell Spout

Danby, Vermont

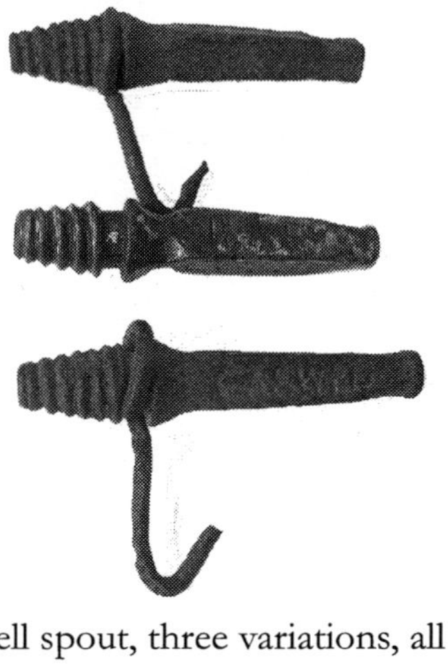

Caswell spout, three variations, all rare

Spout Detective Work -- An experimental Warner spout?

Patents don't necessarily tell the whole story about a spout design. Having a patent did not mean that the inventor stopped trying out new design variations. That probably explains an interesting Warner spout that we found recently.

The upper spout is clearly marked 1893 and matches the patent drawing. It has two inlet holes at the apex. One runs side-to-side across the apex and one is in the end of the apex. It is quite slender.

The middle spout is clearly a Warner spout. However, it is heavier and bigger all around, has just one inlet at the end of the apex, and most interesting, has raised lettering on the bottom that reads:

JIM
SPOUT
IMP'D
PAT.
1893

The M is marred by a casting flaw. It looks to us as if sap flow in the original 1893 design was not good enough, and Warner was experimenting to improve (IMP'D) it. The vertical spout on the right shows the "Jim spout" lettering.

On the bottom spout, there are two inlet holes: one in the end of the apex and one in the bottom. We think that this became the design for the 1899 patent.

1893 patent

1893 patent (improved)

1899 patent

1893 patent (improved), view of bottom

Section Four

MASSACHUSETTS SPOUTS

Mark Hays
1865 Patent

Worcester, Massachusetts

M. HAYS.

Sap-Spout.

No. 45,996. Patented Jan. 24, 1865.

Fig. 1.

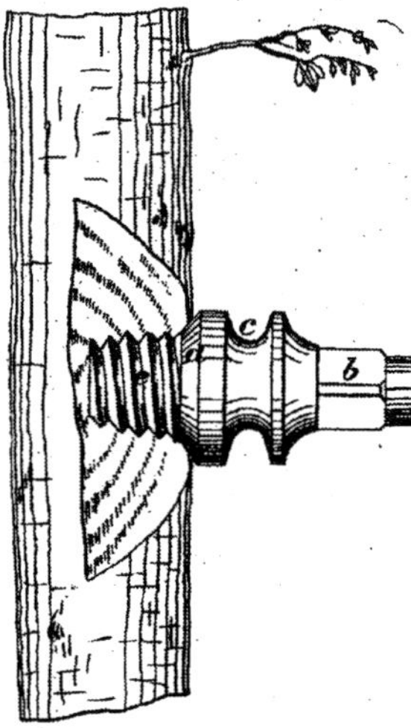

Fig. 2.

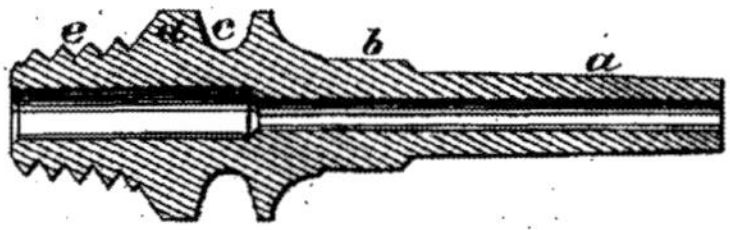

Witnesses:

Theo Tusch

Wm Trewin

Inventor:

Mark Hays

per Munn & Co

Attys.

AM. PHOTO-LITHO. CO. N.Y. (OSBORNE'S PROCESS)

Carleton Barnett
1925 Patent

Cambridge, Massachusetts

Two variations of the Barnett spout

The bottom spout is of heavier construction.

Barnett spouts were sometimes called "harness spouts" or "dandy spouts" because the curved, ball-capped hook on the top resembles the top of a harness hame.

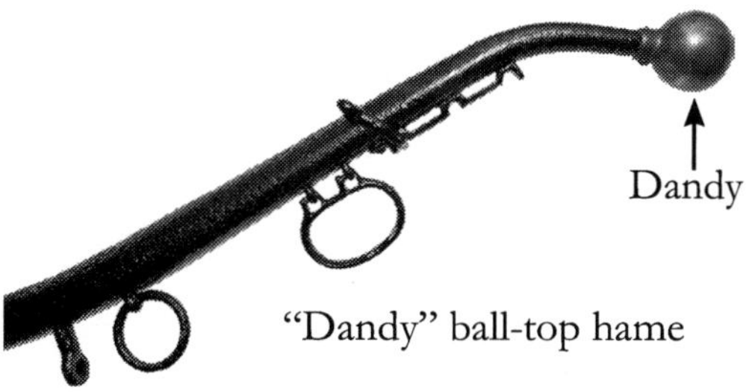

"Dandy" ball-top hame

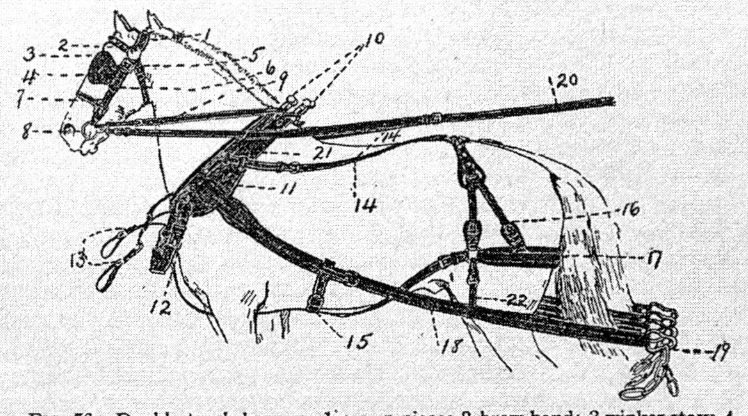

FIG. 56. Double truck harness: 1 crown-piece; 2 brow-band; 3 winker stay; 4 Concord blind; 5 throat-latch; 6 check-piece; 7 nose-band; 8 bit; 9 flat-side rein; 10 "Dandy" ball-top hames; 11 Concord bolt; 12 breast strap; 13 martingales; 14 forked back strap; 15 belly-band; 16 hip straps; 17 breeching; 18 traces; 19 heel chains; 20 lines; 21 leather collar; 22 lazy strap.

George Cady
1869 Patent

Lowell, Massachusetts

Two variations, 3 ⅝" long

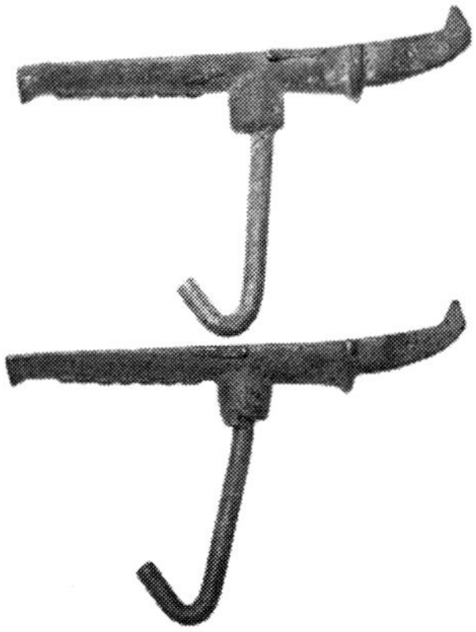

Note difference in apexes.

Seven different patent date configurations, 3 ¼" long

Date "1869" is printed correctly.

Numbers 6 and 9 are reversed.

Section Five

CONNECTICUT SPOUTS

J. B. Sargent
1868 Patent
New Haven, Connecticut

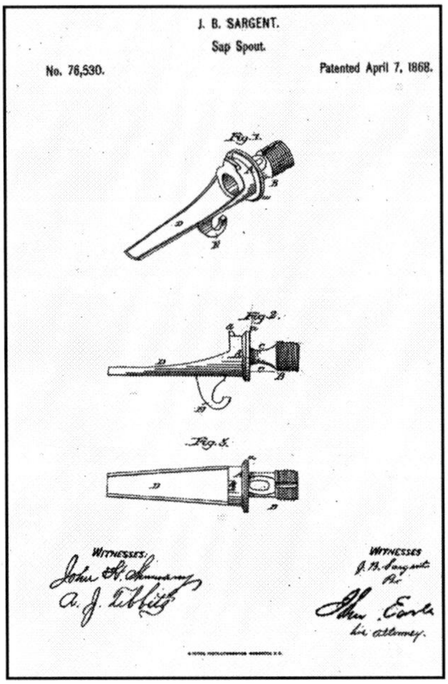

F. O. Mitchell
1892 Patent
Middletown, Connecticut

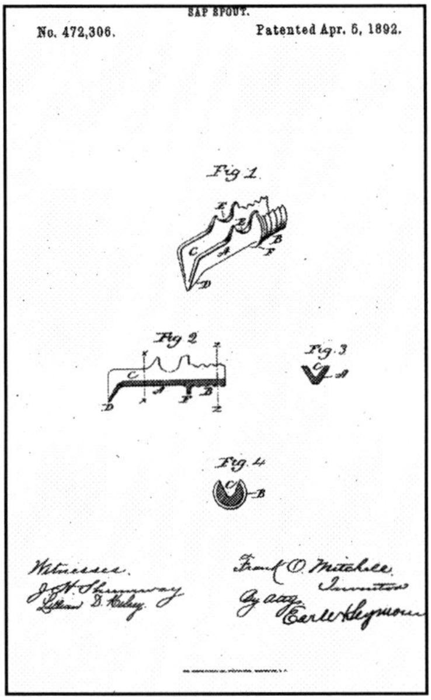

Section Six

NEW HAMPSHIRE SPOUTS

Perley E. Fox
1883 Patent

Marlow, New Hampshire

This spout was sometimes called the Pearl Metallic spout.

Stamped letters on bottom, PATD AUG.8 1883

Two variations of the Fox spout with date running in reversed directions on the bottom

Albert Wood
1893 Patent

Hanover, New Hampshire
(Rare)

This spout could be driven in but needed a wrench for removal from the tap hole.

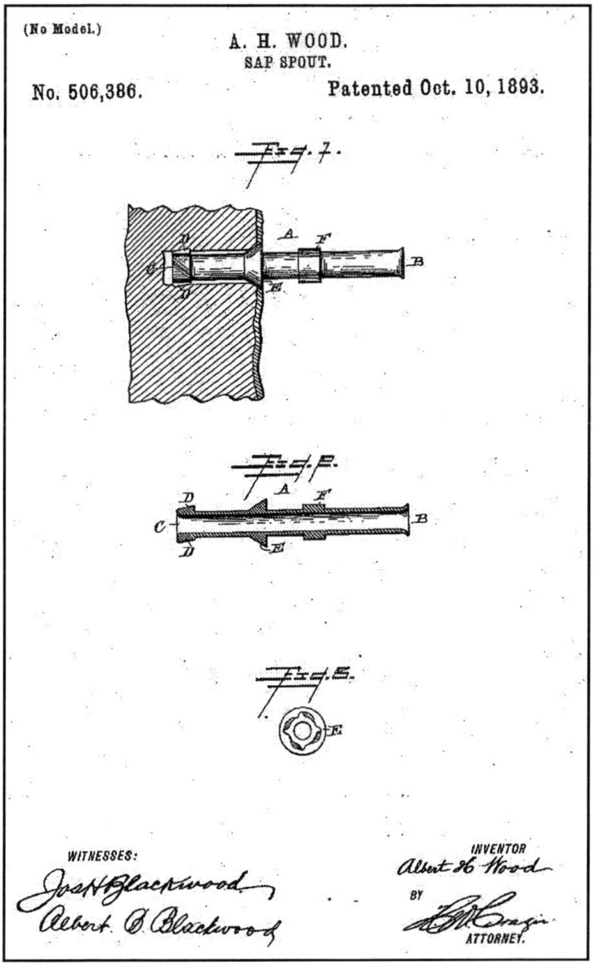

Section Six

MAINE SPOUTS

H. B Sevey
1873 Patent
Vienna, Maine

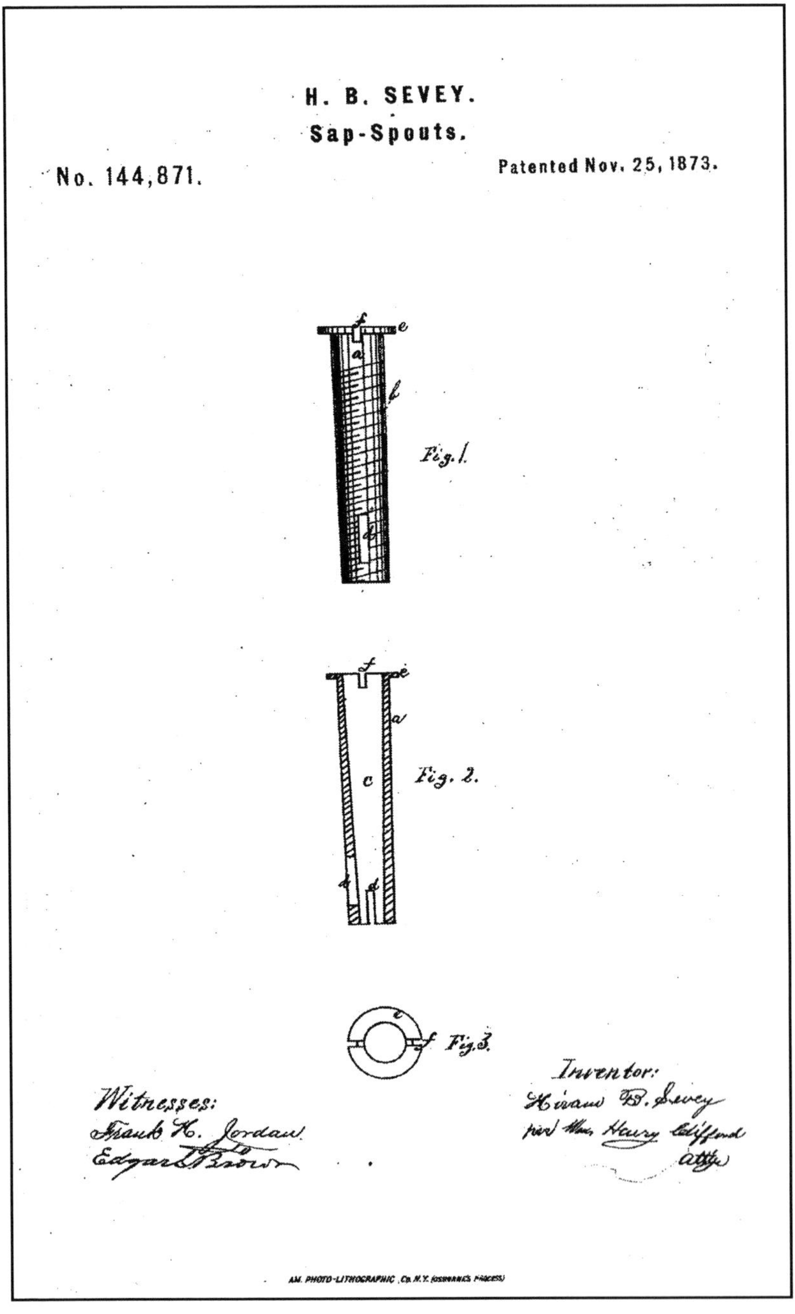

Section Eight

NEW YORK SPOUTS

Homer Hecox
1860 Patent

Rutland, New York

Believed to be the first patented cast spout

Four variations of the Hecox spout

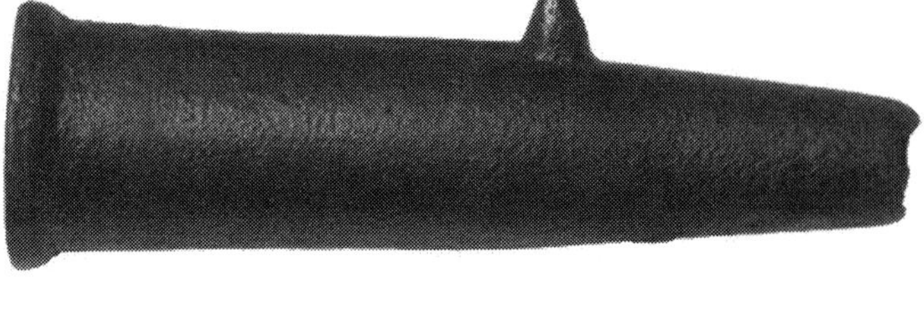

Michael Stark
1882 Patent
Buffalo, New York

Michael Stark was assigner to George Record of Ohio. This is usually called the Record Spout (See page 80).

Christopher Mattice
1885 Patent
Delhi, New York

Many variations in apex and inlet holes, length 2 ¾" to 3 ¼"

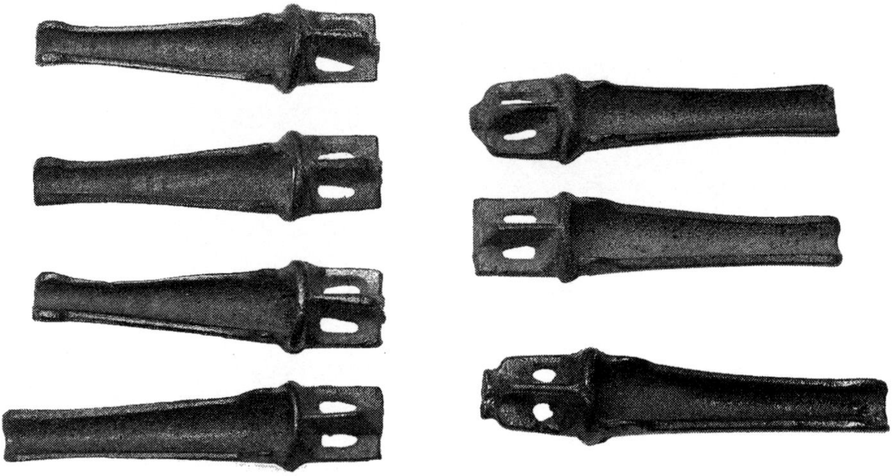

Charles Burr
1887 Patent

Rockdale, New York

Four variations of the Burr spout

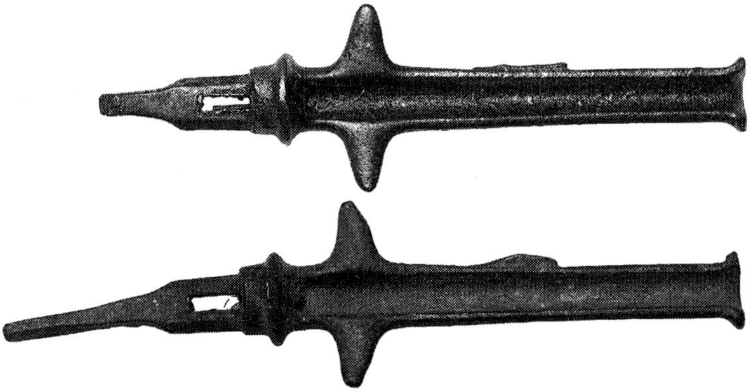

14 VERMONT FARM MACHINE COMPANY, BELLOWS FALLS, VT.

Burr Sap Spouts.

This spout is constructed of iron, tin coated and is strong and durable. It has advantages that make it very desirable.

The end that drives into the tree is enlongated so that it is driven into the body of the tree, which holds it securely; at the same time does not injure the tree or split the bark.

Many thousands are in use, giving excellent satisfaction.

Price per 100, - - - - - - - - - - $2.50.

Eben Willis
1877 Patent
Colton, New York

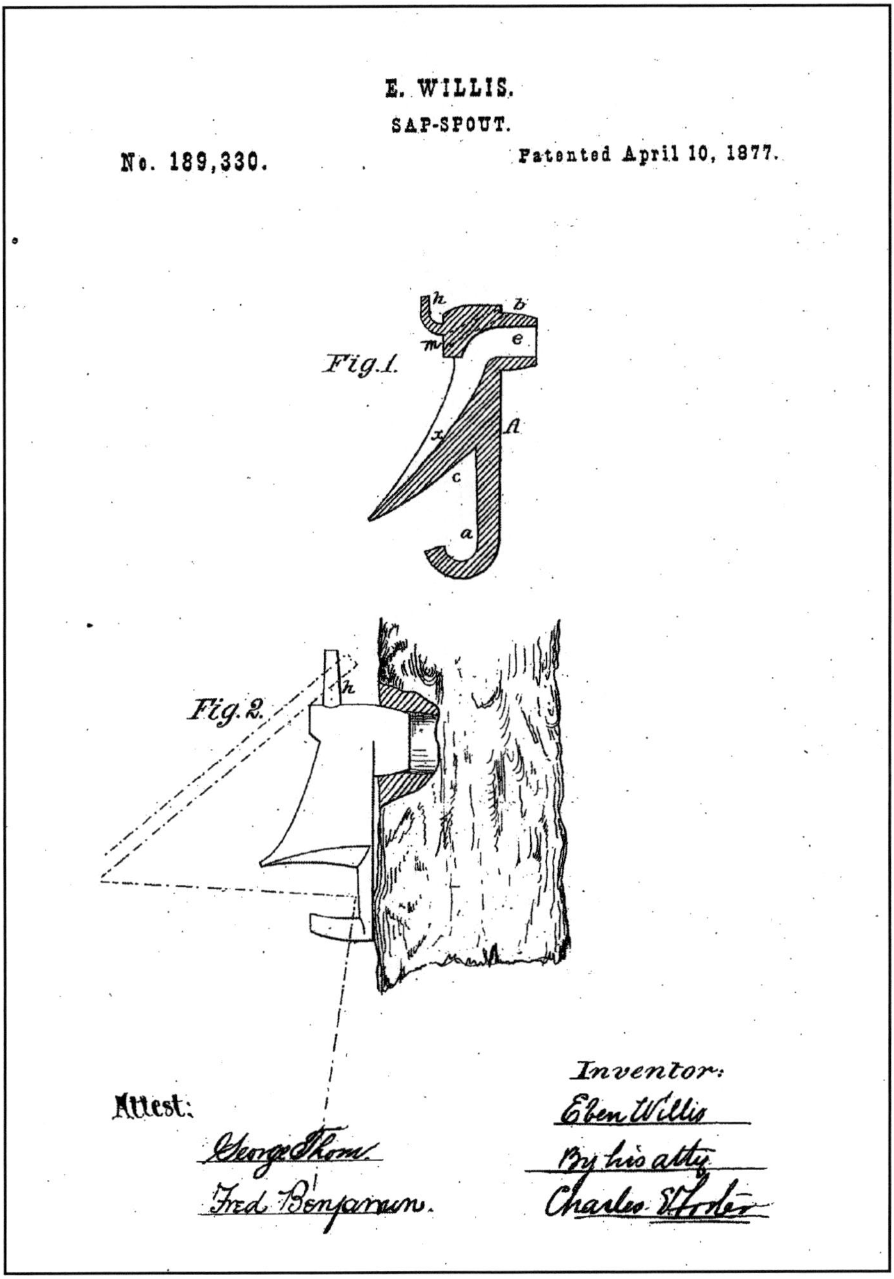

Eben Willis, 1877 Patent, continued, variations

Raised letters, 1877

solid barrel, iron,
2 ⅛" long

open barrel, iron,
2 ¼" long

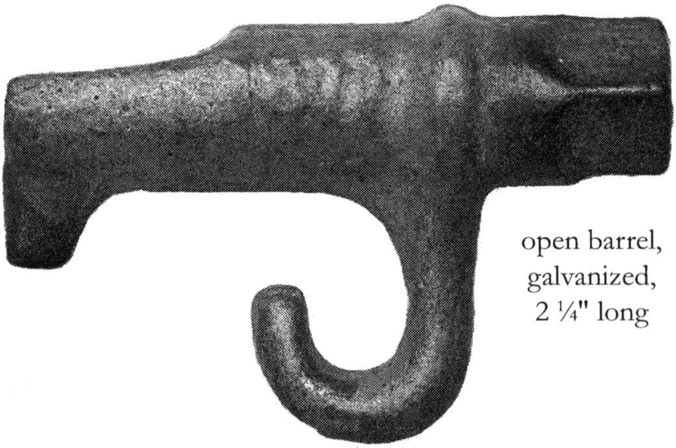

open barrel,
galvanized,
2 ¼" long

Eben Willis
1891 Patent
Colton, New York

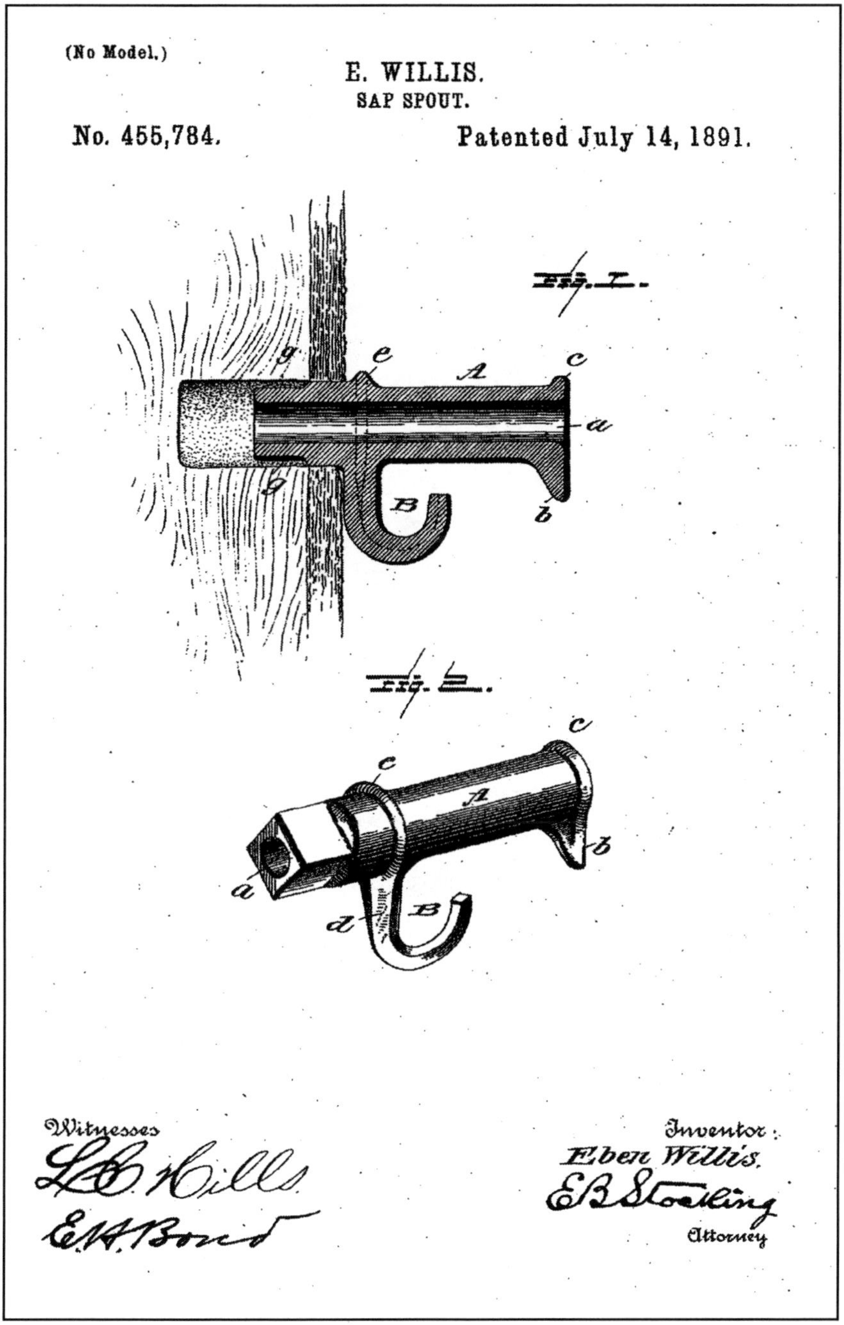

Eben Willis, 1891 Patent, continued

Open barrel; iron or galvanized, length 1 15/16" to 2 1/8"

Raised letters, solid barrel, iron, skeleton apex, 2 ⅛" long, PAT D showing, with 1891 on reverse

Raised date showing, open barrel, iron, square apex, 2 ⅛" long, PAT D on reverse

Raised date showing, open barrel, iron, skeleton apex, 2 ⅛" long, PAT D on reverse

Raised date, open barrel, iron, arched, skeleton apex, 2 1/16" long, PAT D on reverse

No lettering, solid barrel, iron, skeleton apex, 2 3/16" long

Eben Willis
1898 Patent
Colton, New York

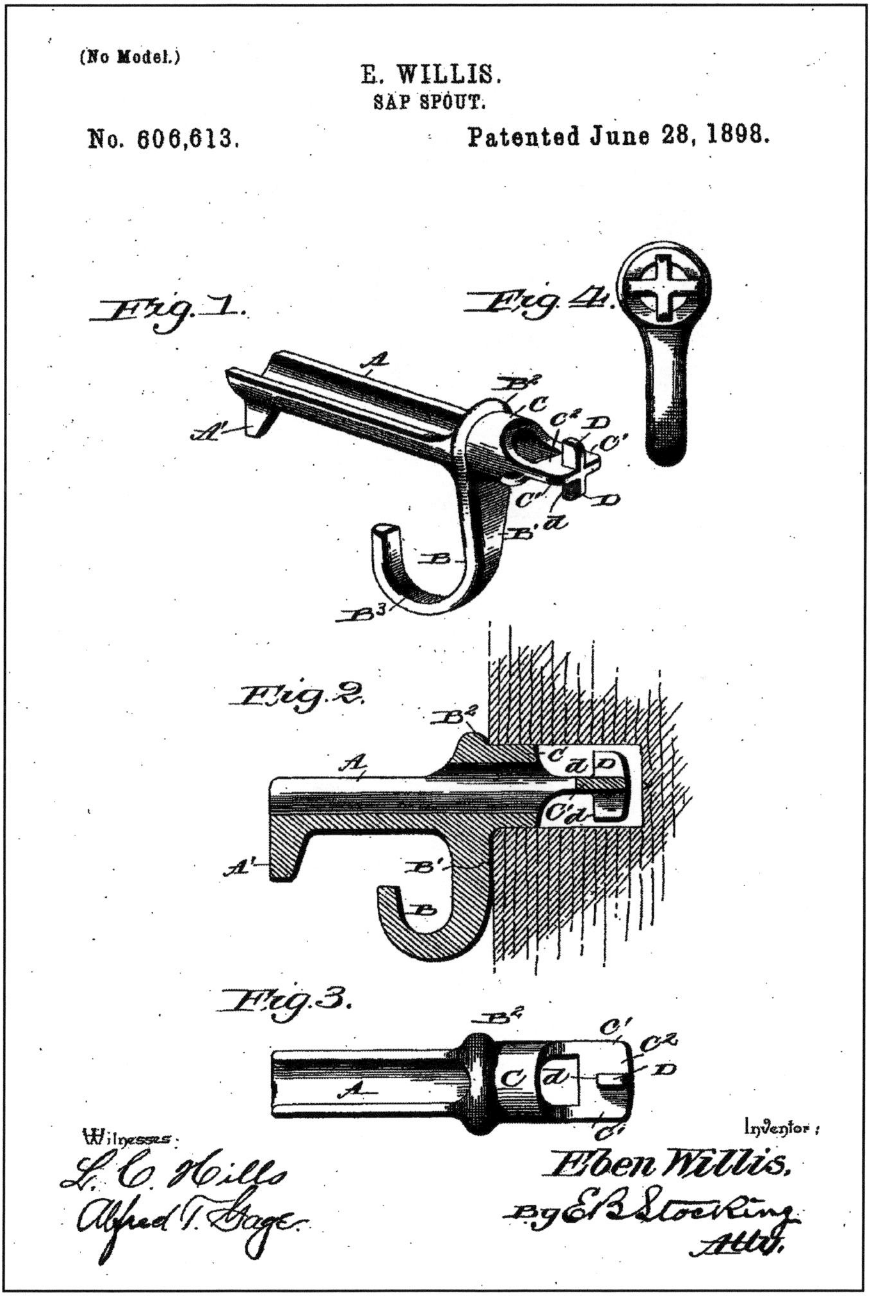

Eben Willis, 1898 Patent, continued

Raised date showing, open barrel, iron, skeleton apex, PAT D on reverse; length from 2 1/8" to 2 7/16"

arched

slightly arched

Raised PAT D showing, solid barrel, iron, skeleton apex, date on reverse; length from 2 ⅛" to 2 ½"

Charles Miller & Son Company
Ideal Sap Spout

Utica, New York

THE
IDEAL SAP SPOUT.

OPEN TOP.

THE
IDEAL SAP SPOUT.

CLOSED TOP.

Both kinds are very handsomely finished, and are made to fit a hole bored with a half-inch bit.

Dealers will find it most decidedly to their advantage to confine their sales exclusively to these desirable spouts.

Send in your orders early so that you may have the goods when they are needed.

PRICES TO DEALERS.

No. 1 Tinned Open Top, per 100, net	$1.05
No. 1 Tinned Closed Top, per 100, net.....	1.15

Charles Millar & Son Co.,
Sole Manufacturers,
UTICA, N. Y.

Four variations of the Ideal Sap Spout

Solid barrels

Open barrels

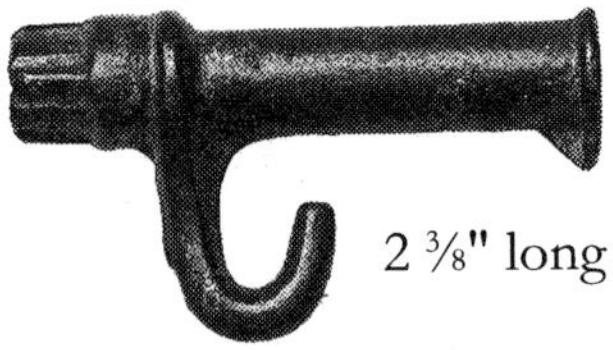

2 ⅜" long

2 ⅜" long

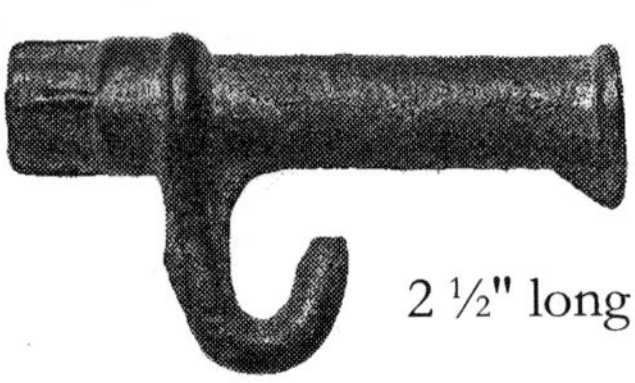

2 ½" long

2 ½" long

William C. Brower
1915 Patent (USA)
1917 Patent (Canada)

Cranberry Creek, New York

Brower spouts were part of the Brower Sap Piping System described on the following page.

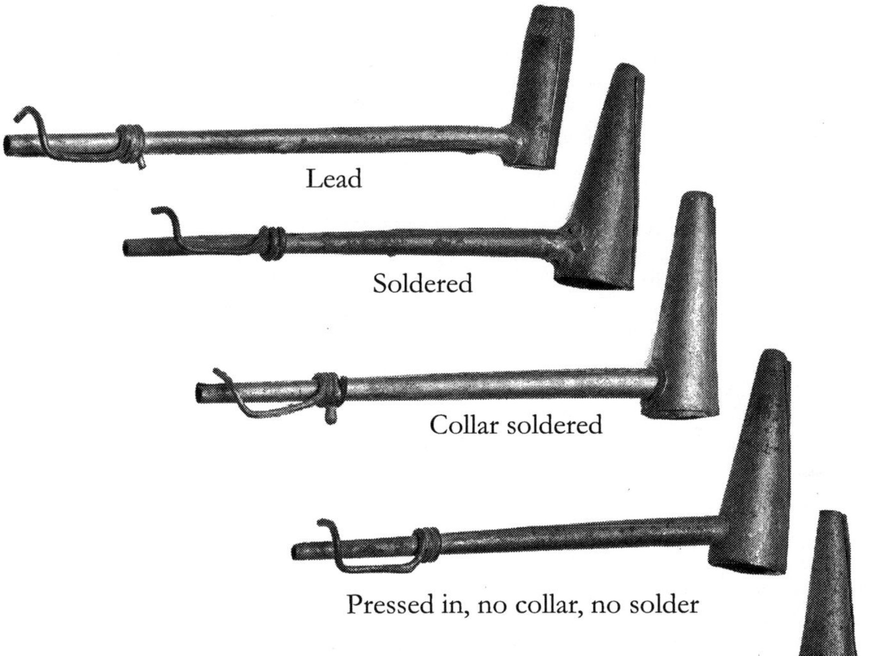

Lead

Soldered

Collar soldered

Pressed in, no collar, no solder

Smaller stem with only a single wrap of the spring lock (as opposed to several wraps) on the stem

The Brower Sap Piping System
Patented
In U.S. Dec. 17th, 1915
In Canada June 12th, 1917

The Brower System is the invention of William C. Brower of Cranberry Creek, New York.

Mr. Brower was a tinsmith by trade and also owned a sugar orchard which was located on one of the steep hills of the Adirondack region.

One night about ten years years ago, after a hard day's work carrying sap through the deep snow, being wet to the skin, discouraged, and thoroughly tired out, he went to bed trying to think of some plan which would do away with the hard disagreeable work of sugar making.

As Mr. Brower was an inventive genius, he, in time thought out a plan by which the sap might be piped direct from the trees to the sugar house. From this plan grew the idea which has resulted in the present Brower Piping System.

Like all great inventions, this had a very humble beginning. Mr. Brower, began the manufacture and sale of his piping system over ten years ago in his home town in New York state.

Knowing that Mr. Cary was one of the largest sugar makers of the country, he came to St. Johnsbury to try to sell him an outfit for one of his sugar orchards. Mr. Cary did not consider the idea at all practical and would not buy it, but finally, Mr. Brower persuaded him to take enough for 1500 trees on trial. After using this one year, Mr. Cary bought an equipment for 9000 more trees and at present is using it on over 15000 trees.

The Cary Maple Sugar Company, realizing that this system would help to make more and better sugar, with a greatly reduced cost in production, agreed to finance the manufacture of the Brower Sap Piping System on a much larger scale than ever before attempted, and Mr. Brower moved to St. Johnsbury, Vermont, to personally superintend the work. The first year, the business was more than doubled and at present the Company is not able to manufacture the piping as fast as the orders are received. This has been brought about entirely by the merits of the system as no advertising has been done. Small trial orders always result in larger reorders and many new orders from people who have watched the first try-out of the system. We know of no better recommendation than this.

Taken from an instruction booklet for the system, probably published in the late teens of the 20th century

Section Nine

MICHIGAN SPOUTS

Eli Mosher
1860 Patent
Flushing, Michigan

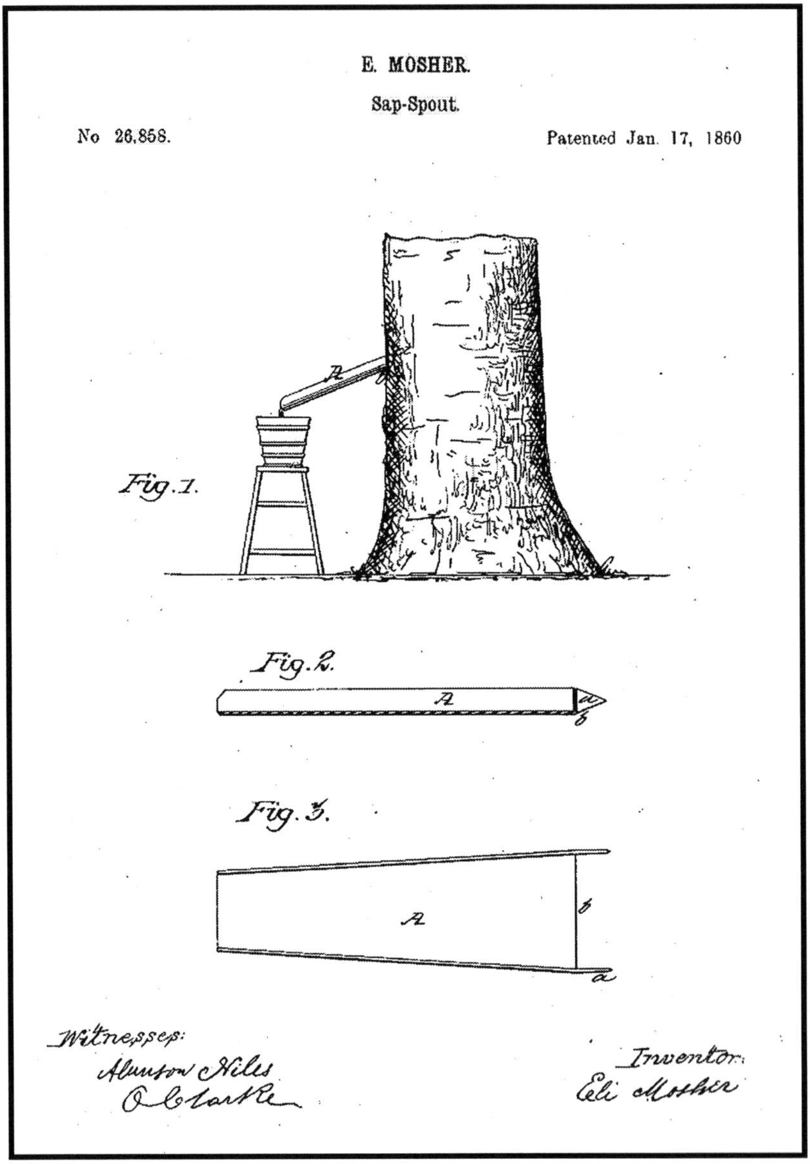

The Mosher spout is thought to be the first metal spout patented.

Section Ten

OHIO SPOUTS

George J. Record
1882 Patent
Conneaut, Ohio

Three variations of the Record spout

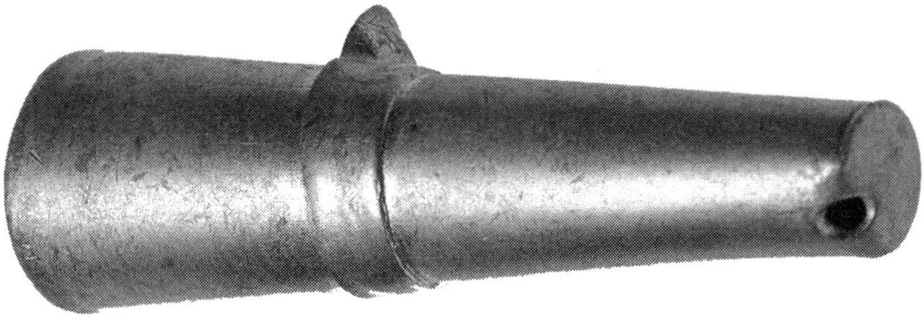

This is the 1882 spout that Stark assigned to Record.

George J. Record
1895 Patent

Conneaut, Ohio

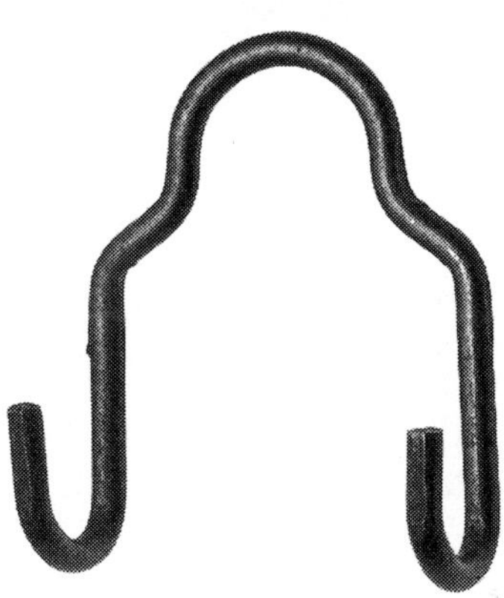

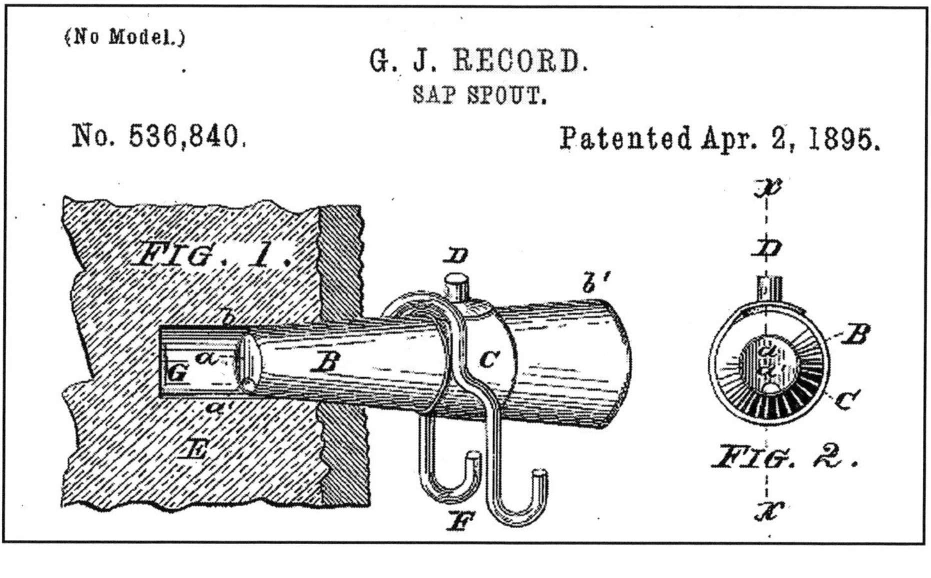

Alexander B. Kilpatrick
1903 Patent

Warren, Ohio

The Kilpatrick patent

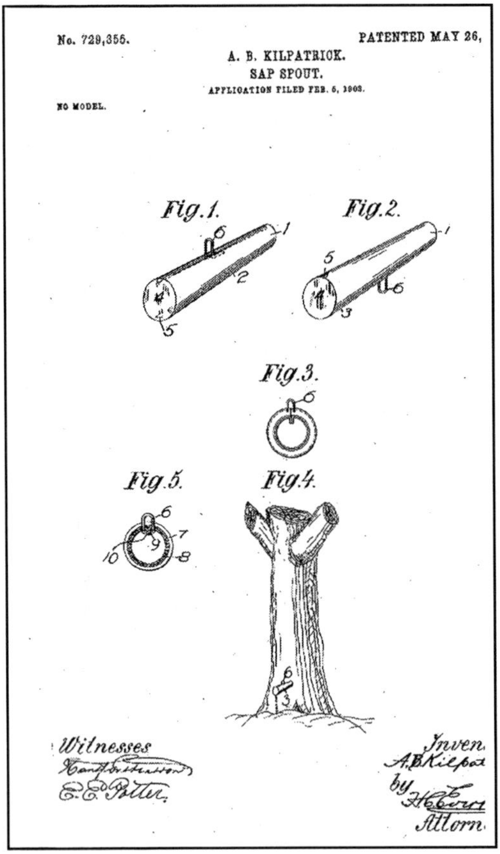

The three spouts below may also be Kilpatrick spouts.

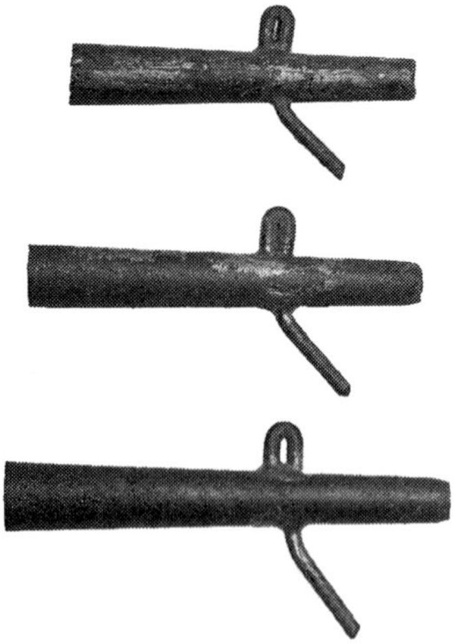

Section Eleven

ILLINOIS SPOUTS

Augustin Ring
1898 Patent

Fisher, Illinois

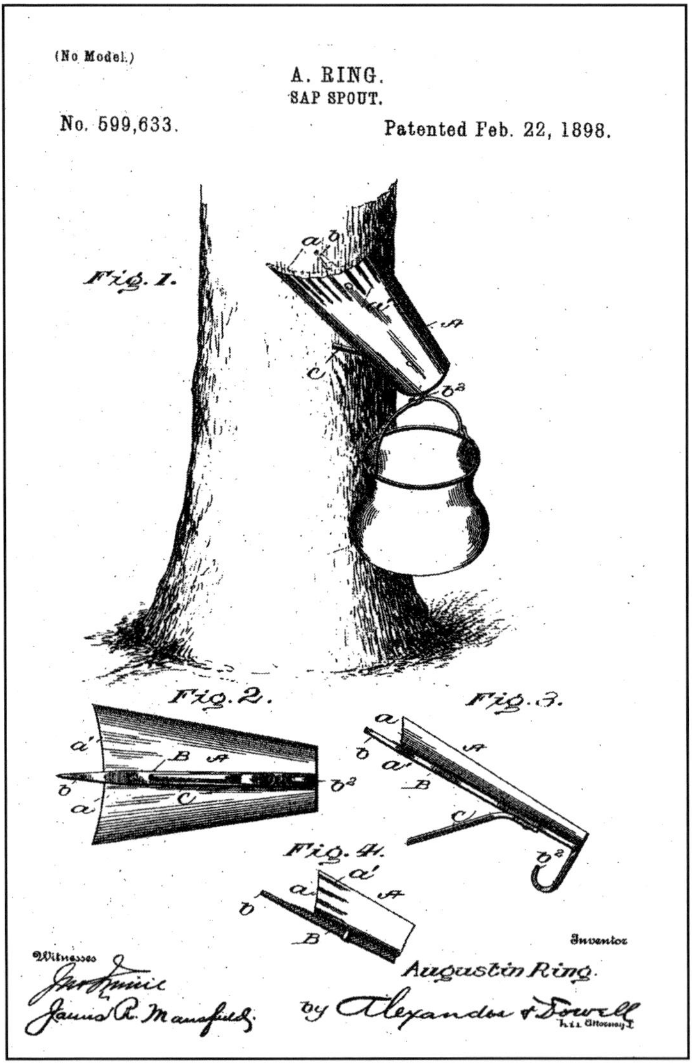

John O'Connor
1908 Patent
Chicago, Illinois

These spouts are highly sought after by collectors because of their unusual characteristics.

Early version

Later version

See patent next page

John O'Connor, 1908 Patent, continued

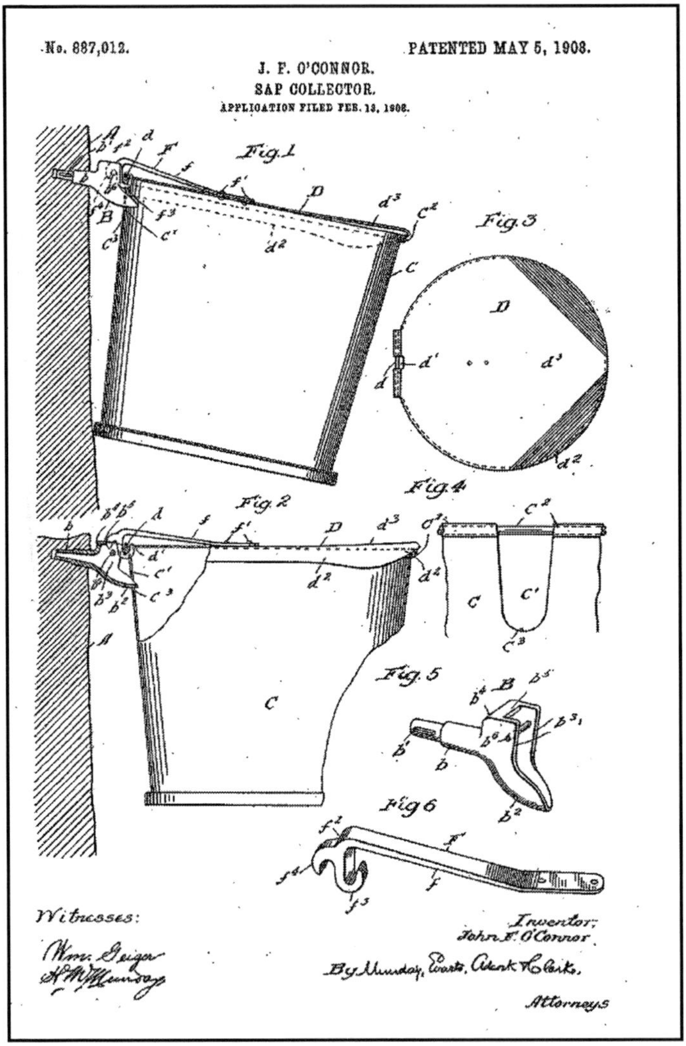

Section Twelve

CANADIAN SPOUTS

Alford Goodson
1882 Patent
Bastard, Ontario, Canada

Two variations of the Goodson spout

Goodson spout and tool used to insert and remove it

H. A. & Z. S. Laurence
1882 Patent
West Shefford, Québec, Canada

James Davidson
1895 Patent
Montréal, Québec, Canada

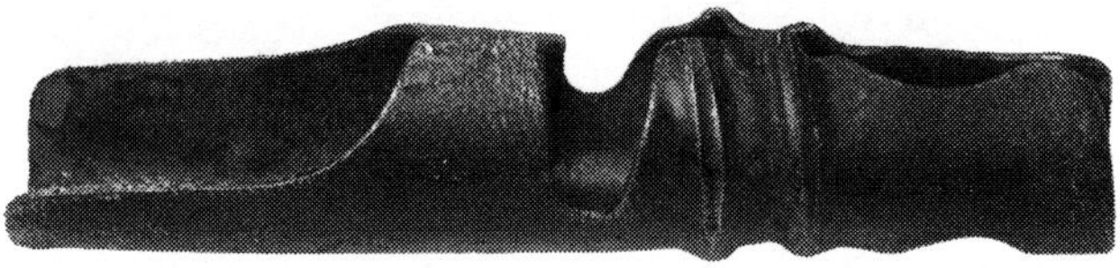

William McDonald
1893 Patent
Granby, Québec, Canada

Date reads 5/30/1893, but patent date is 3/20/1893

William McDonald
1910 Patent
Granby, Québec, Canada

Canadian Lightning Spout
No patent found

Series 1
Numbered 1-10

Series 2
Lettered A-Z

Series 3
Numbered 1-10 Z

Series 4
Lettered A-Z Z

These spouts are known to come in two apex styles:

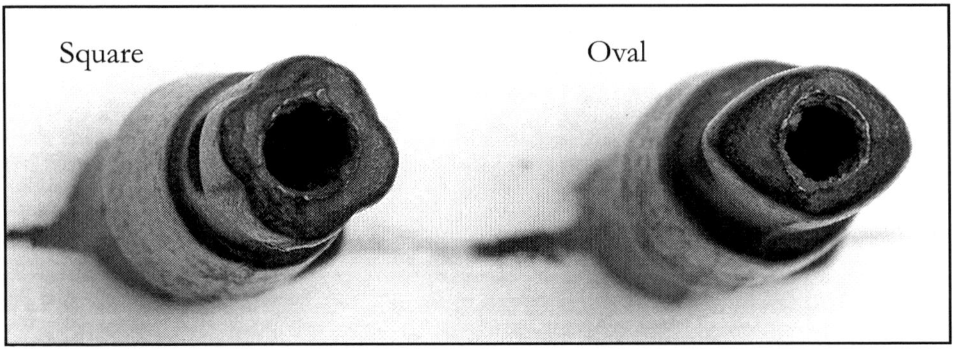

This family of spouts has an unknown number of variations.

Sylva LeBrun
1955 Patent
Canada

Two variations of the LeBrun aluminum alloy spout

Booster Spout
No patent found

The Booster Spout, made in the early 1900's, is a very unusual type of cast spout. The sap ran down the attached wire into a vessel below the tap hole. This spout allowed sap from several taps on a large sugar maple to flow into one vessel.

L'Hoir Spout

Lévis, Québec, Canada

Advertisement, around 1950

Unidentified spouts similar to the Royal Spout

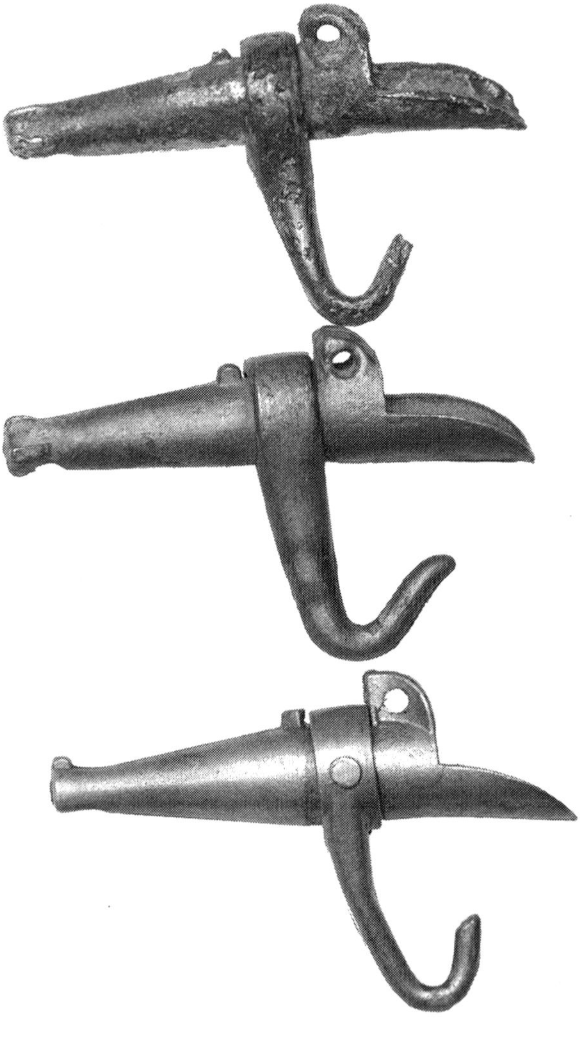

These are mystery spouts. We believe they are Canadian.

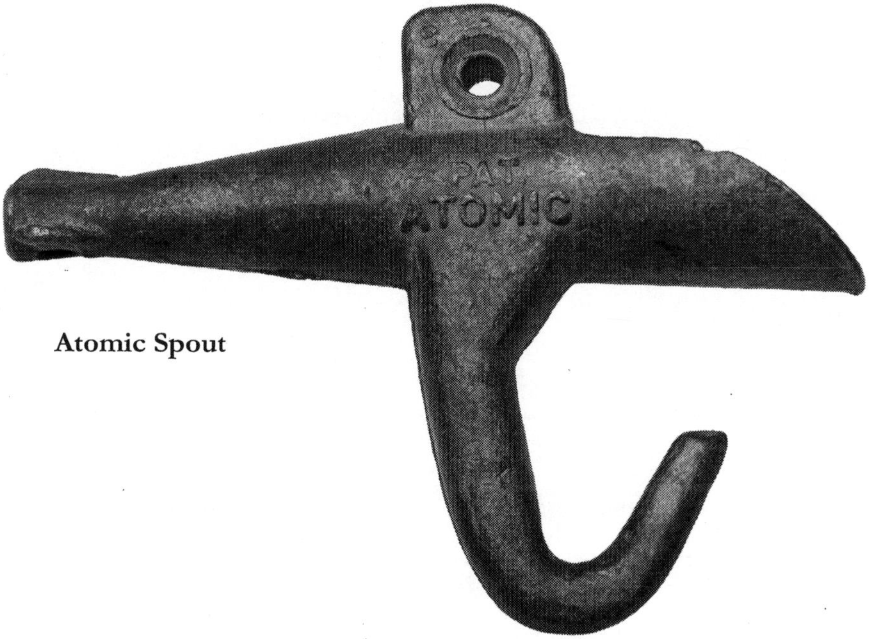

Atomic Spout

Modern Canadian Spouts

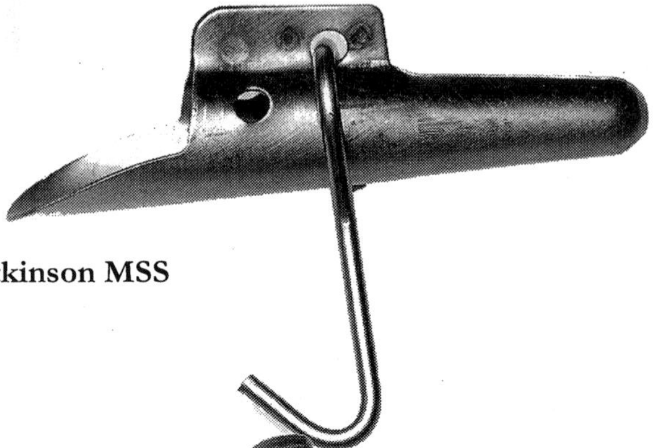

Atkinson MSS

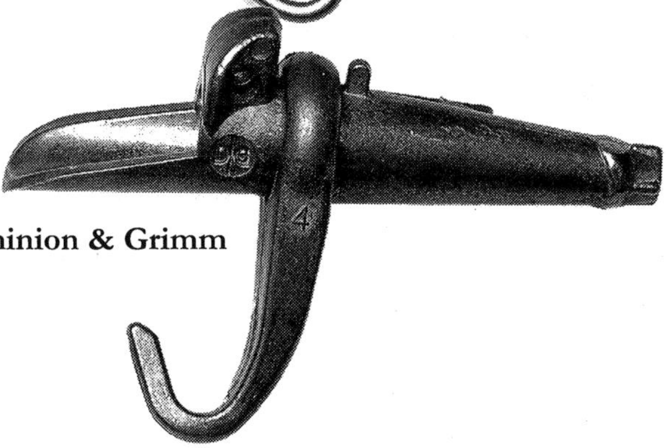

Dominion & Grimm

Canadian Leader Health Spout

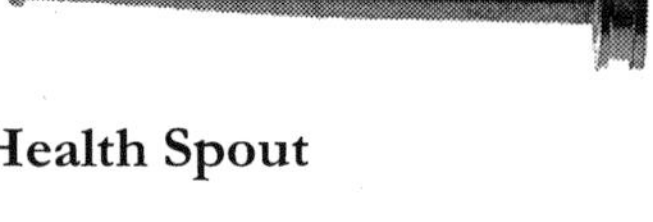

CDL Stainless Health Spout

Plastic Canadian Spouts

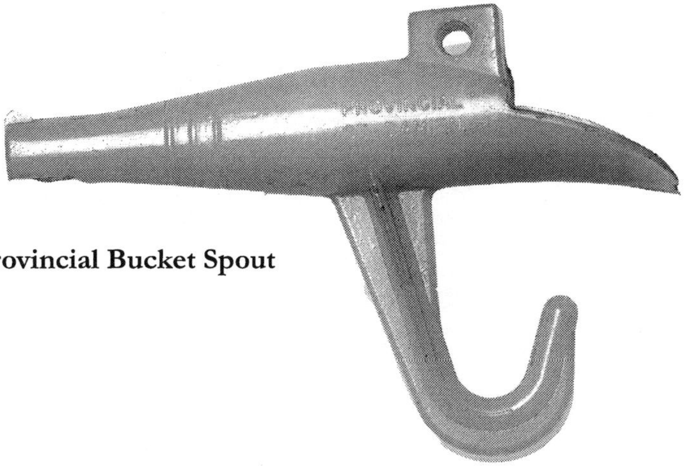

Provincial Bucket Spout

Spouts for flexible pipeline

Left, top to bottom:

IPL Canadian 93
CDL 66090
Lamb #4 Maple
Unknown
Short D&G

Right, top to bottom:

Lamb Plug
D&G Tubing Spout
Unknown
Unknown

Section Thirteen

SPOUTS CURRENTLY BEING RESEARCHED

Grimm type with multiple comb, eye size, and apex inlet variations

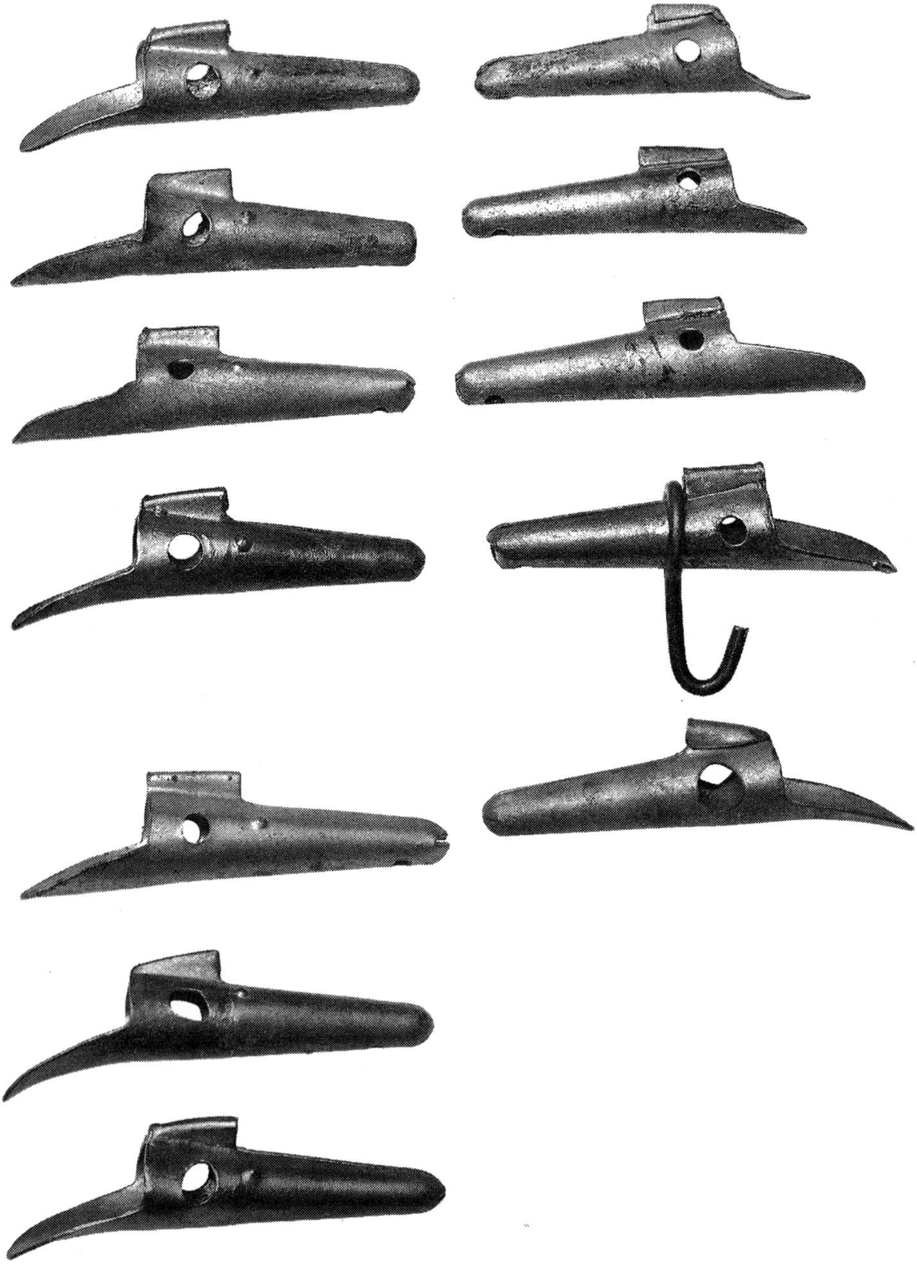

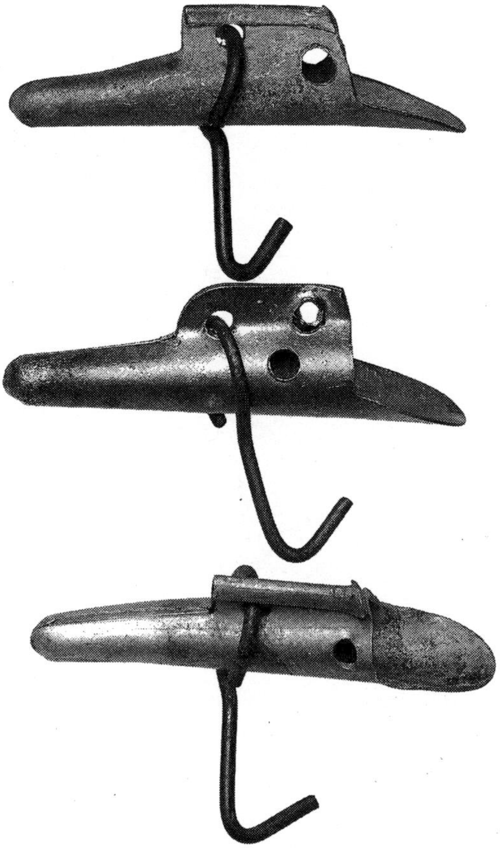

Formed type with multiple variations

F & J Co. No.1 and No.2 with variations in length, inlet hole, and construction

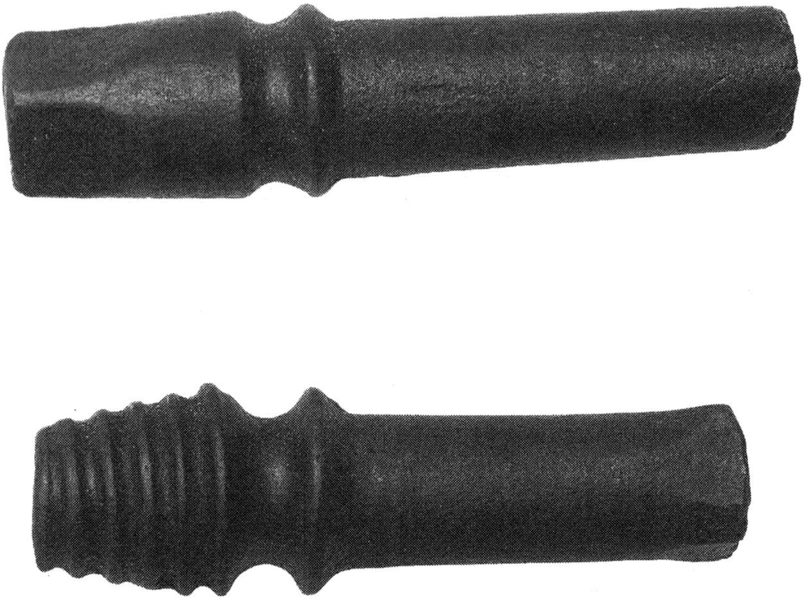

Spouts with Goodson Spout characteristics

Unusual heavy gauge formed sheet metal spout

Both unknown, formed sheet metal

Cannon Spout
This spout is much desired by collectors.

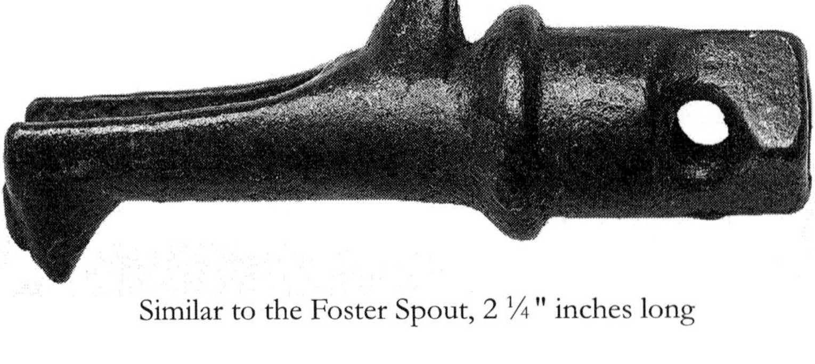

Similar to the Foster Spout, 2 ¼" inches long

These may be homemade spouts.

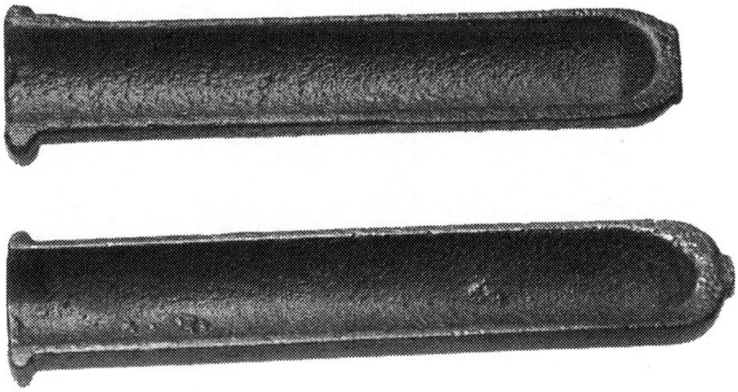

Top and bottom views of open channel spout

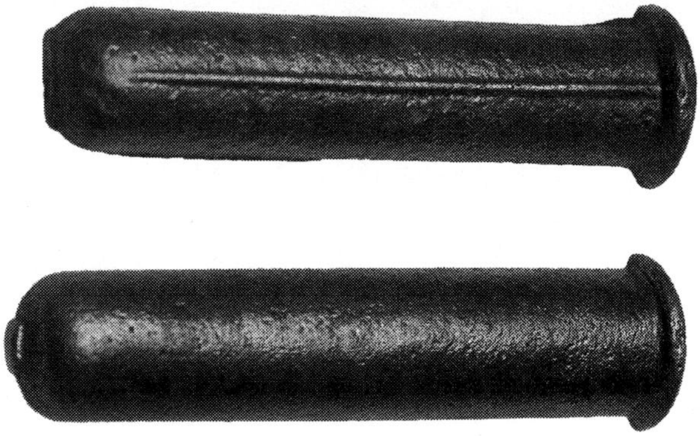

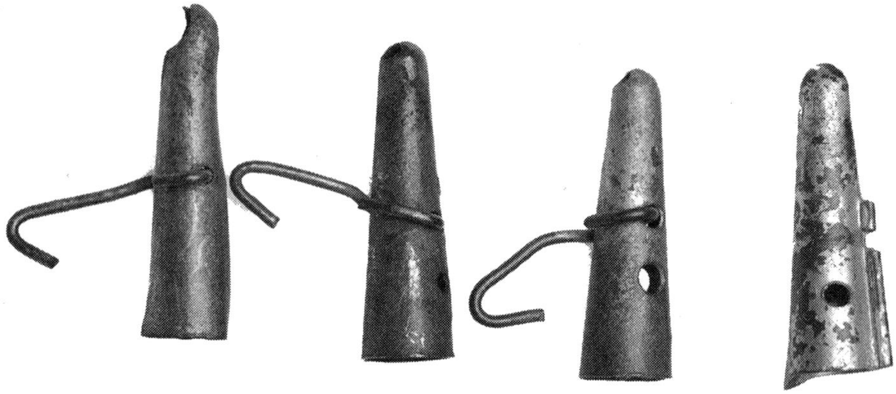

Unknown

Unknown, with unusual hooks and seam formation

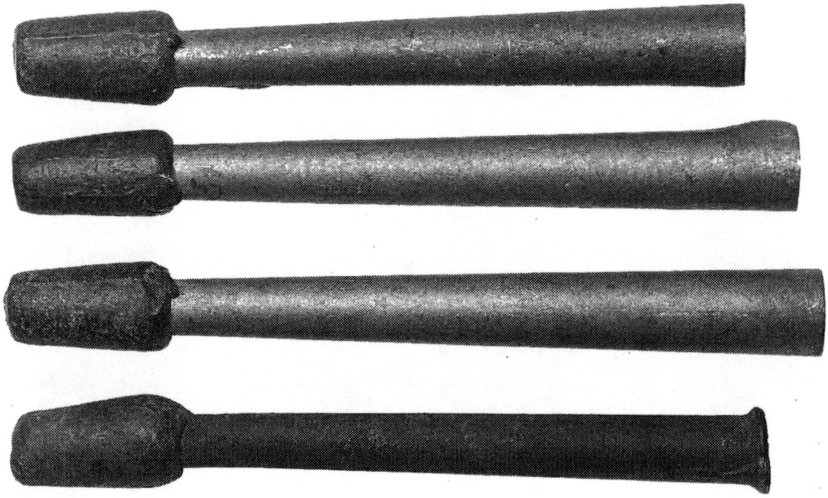

Spouts with leaded apex

Very heavily constructed cast iron spout,
sometimes called the **Grudge Spout**

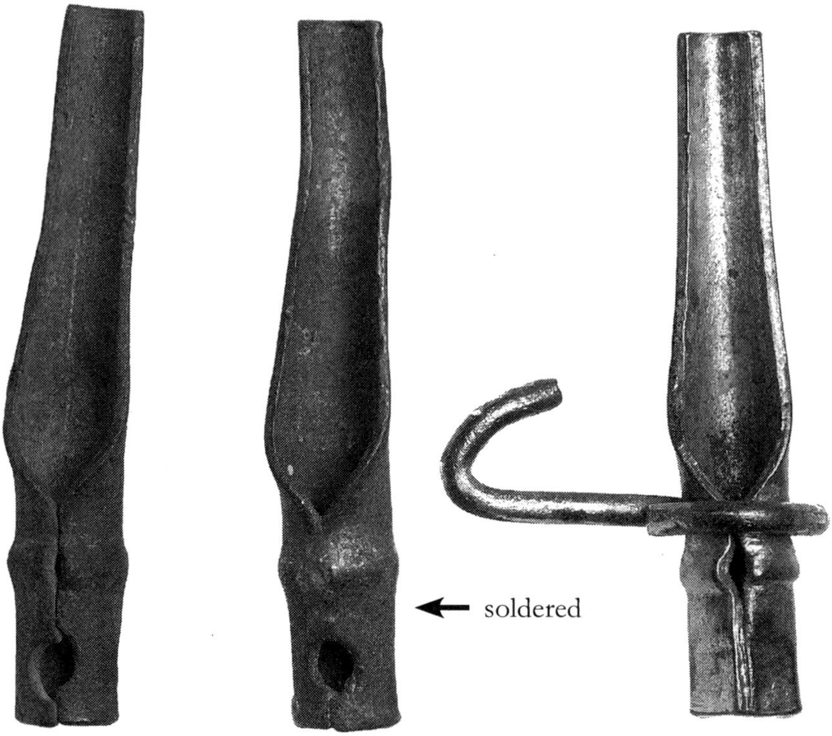

Cooley Spout variations

Robbins Spout

Similar to the Warner Spout but with no identification markings

Three inlet holes

One inlet hole

Two inlet holes

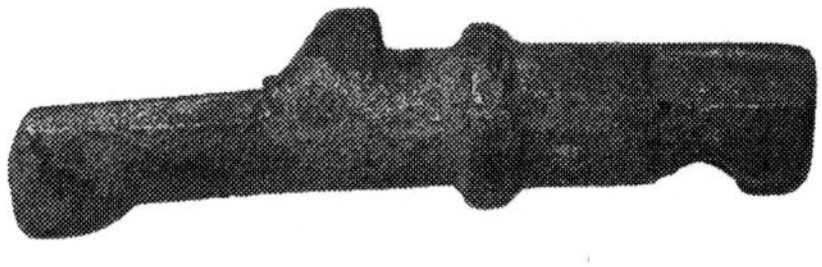

Same as above, but
heavier contrucion

Section Fourteen

ODDITIES

Warner Spouts with casting flaws

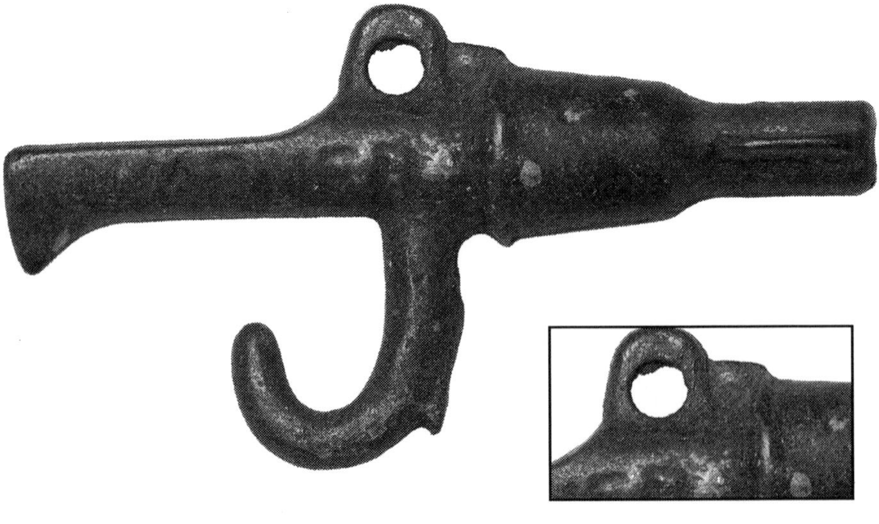

Foster Spouts with flaws

One-eyed **Eureka Spout**

Unknown with swollen lip

Warner Spout with no eye

Warner Spout hit by axe or splitting maul

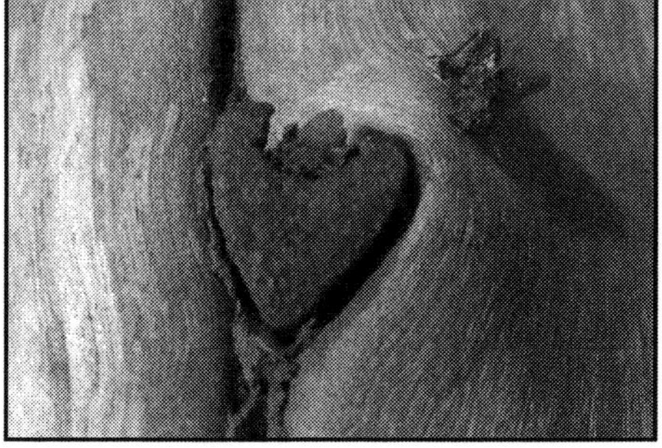

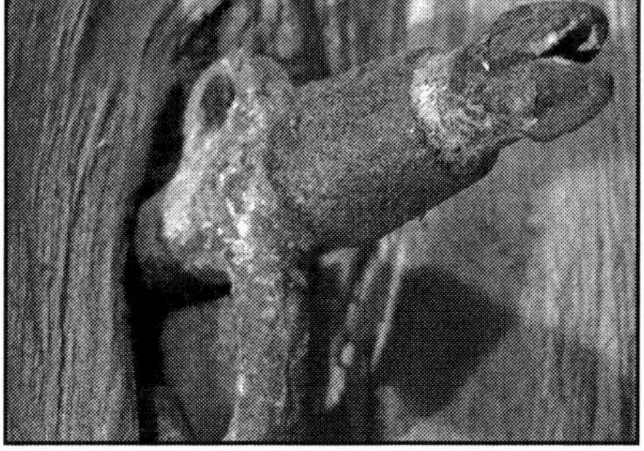

Result of a **Soule Spout** left in a tree

Section Fifteen

METAL HOOKS and TAPPING TOOLS

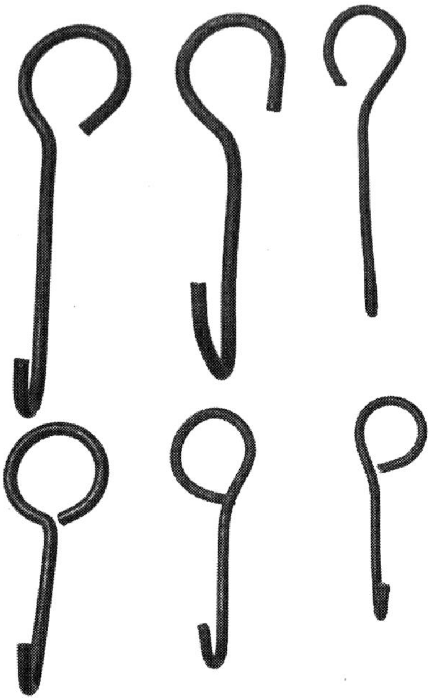

Types of wire hooks used with wood and metal sap spouts

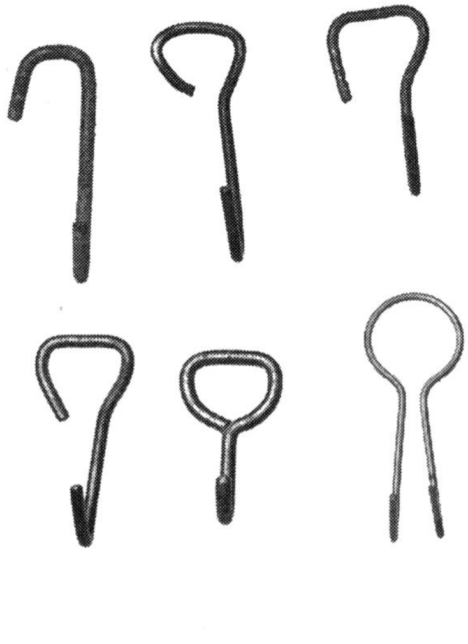

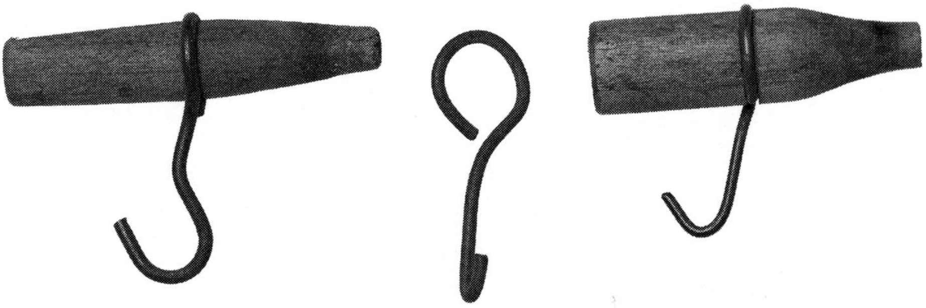

Two wooden spouts with different bucket hooks

Tapping tools

Gouge

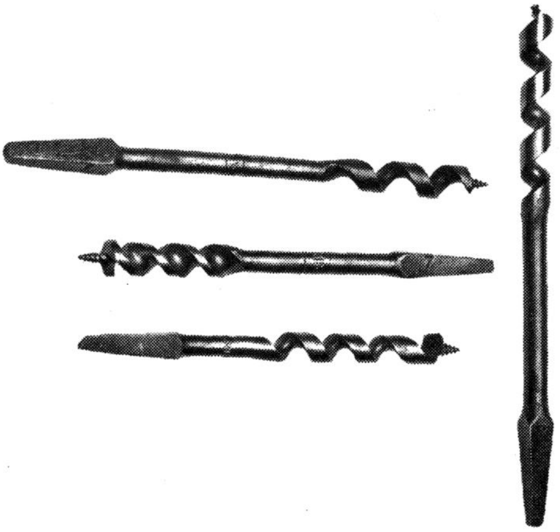

Warner and Grimm tapping bits

(No Model.)

M. R. MOSS.

SAP SPOUT EXTRACTOR.

No. 513,591. Patented Jan. 30, 1894.

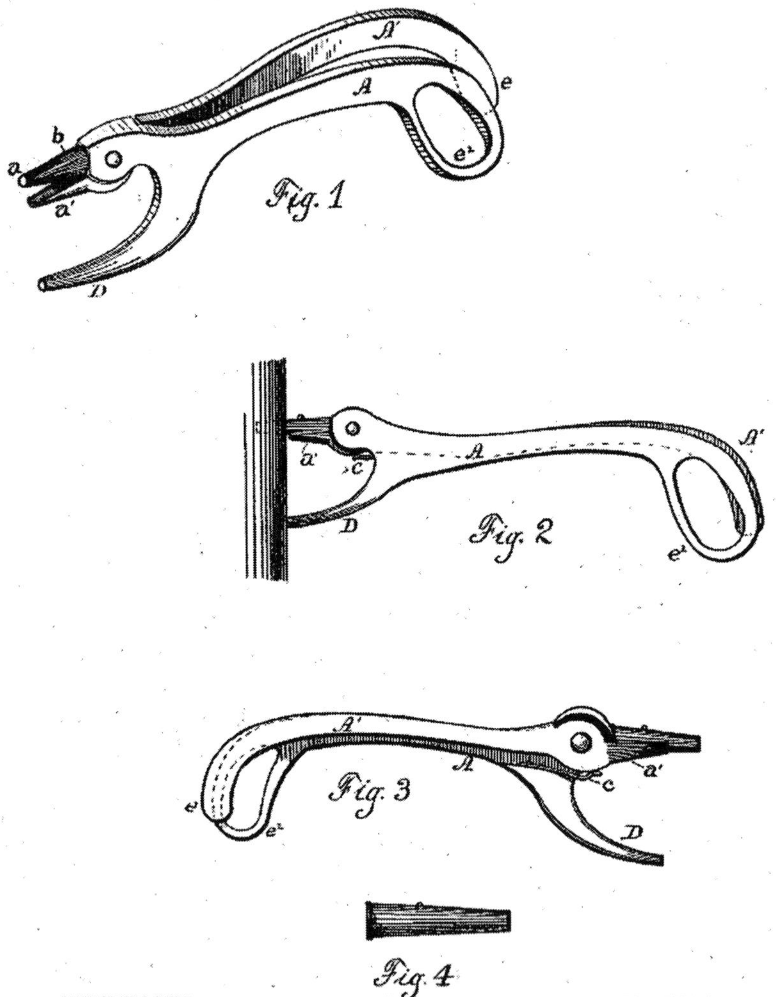

WITNESSES

INVENTOR

Marvin R. Moss

by

ATTORNEY

THE NATIONAL LITHOGRAPHING COMPANY, WASHINGTON, D. C.

(No Model.)

M. R. MOSS.

REAMING BIT.

No. 505,322. Patented Sept. 19, 1893.

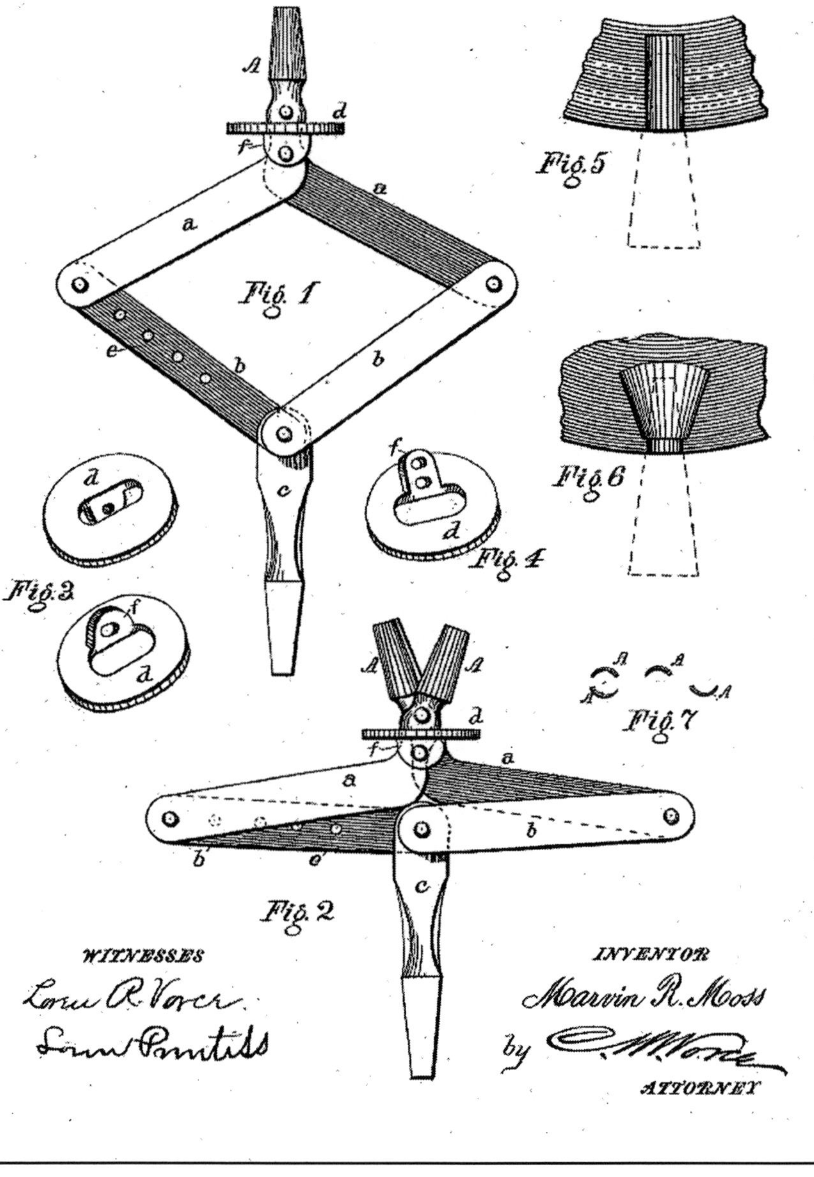

(No Model.)

A. M. FOSTER.

BARK ROSSING DEVICE.

No. 563,584.

Patented July 7, 1896.

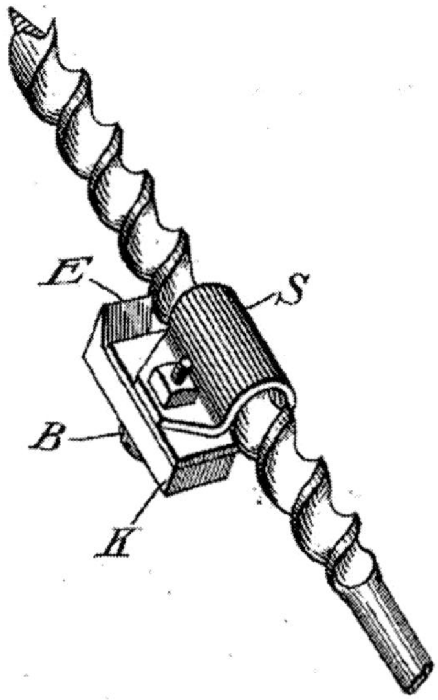

Witnesses.

Frank L. Laird

Louis J. Walbridge

Inventor

Alonzo M. Foster

Section Sixteen

AMERICAN PLASTIC PIPELINE SPOUTS

A few plastic spouts showing design variations

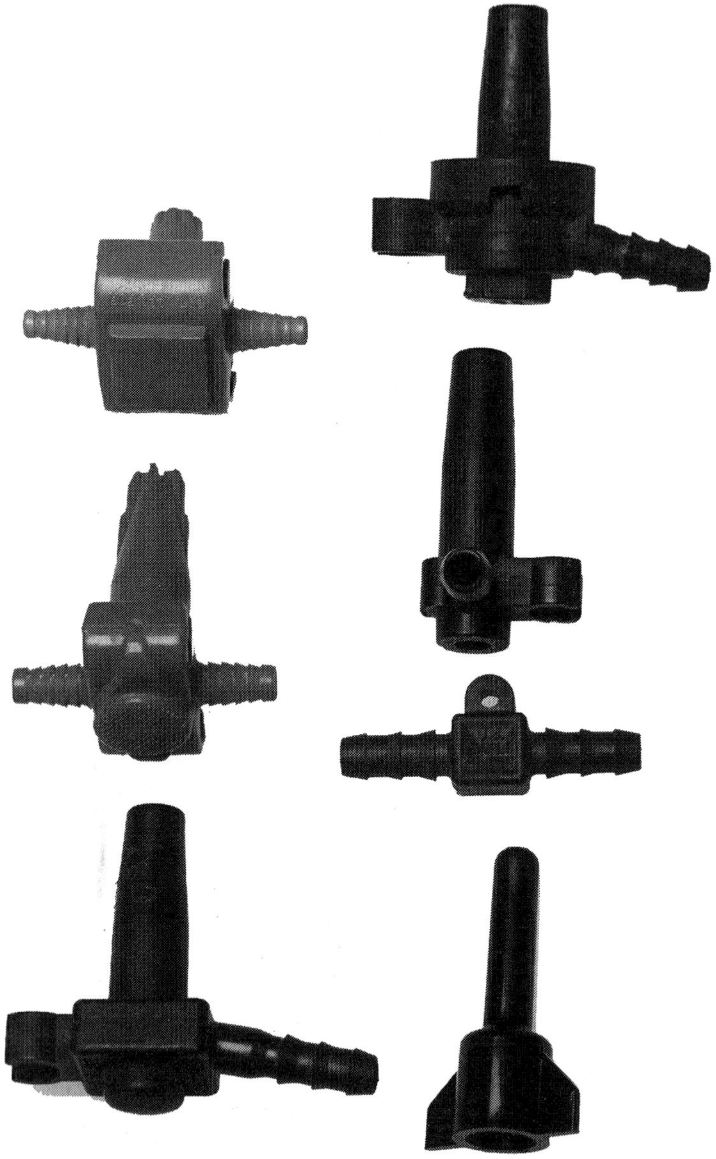

Top to bottom:

Mapleflo
Mapleflo
BP Inc.

Top to bottom:

US Maple
SMI
US Maple Connector
Leader Check Valve